FROM PIECES TO PEACE

FINDING PEACE IN 5 KEY AREAS OF YOUR LIFE

SELONE AJEWOLE

This book is dedicated to anyone who has ever felt to be in pieces yet has had the courage to still pursue peace with everything in them.

This publication has been devised in order to provide competent information on the subject matter at hand. Please note however that this book is sold under the premise that neither the author nor the publisher is engaged in rendering financial or legal advice. Furthermore, both the author and publisher therefore disclaim any liability incurred from the application of the contents of this book.

Copyright © 2018 by 29Eleven Publishing

Cover design by IKB Media Group (www.ikbusari.com)

Photography by Emmanuel Hammond (www.emmanuelhammond.com)

Makeup by Ayo Adegboyega (www.creativechiczhair.com)

The photocopying, scanning, uploading, or distributing of this book without permission is strictly prohibited and is considered theft of the author's intellectual property. If you require permission to use material from this book, please contact hello@29eleven.tv. Your support in protecting the author's rights is much appreciated.

29Eleven Publishing
259 High Street
London
E15 2LS

The publisher does not assume any responsibility for websites that are not owned by the publisher.

First Edition: August 2018

29Eleven Publishers provide varied authors for speaking events. For further information, please contact hello@29eleven.tv.

Scripture quotations marked (NIV) are taken from The Holy Bible, New International Version ®, NIV®, Copyright © 1973, 1978, 1984, 2011 by Biblica, Inc.® Used by permission. All rights reserved worldwide.

Scripture quotations marked (NLT) are taken from the *Holy Bible*, New Living Translation, copyright © 1996, 2004, 2015 by Tyndale House Foundation. Used by permission of Tyndale House Publishers, Inc., Carol Stream, Illinois 60188. All rights reserved.

Scripture quotations marked (KJV) are taken from the *King James Version of the Bible*.

Scripture quotations marked (CEV) are taken from the Contemporary English Version®. Copyright © 1995 American Bible Society. All rights reserved.

Scripture quotations marked (GW) are taken from God's Word ®, copyright © 1995, God's Word to the Nations. Used by permission of Baker Publishing Group.

Scripture quotations marked (MSG) are taken from *The Message*. Copyright © 1993, 1994, 1995, 1996, 2000, 2001, 2002. Used by permission of NavPress Publishing Group.

Scripture quotations marked (ESV) are taken from The Holy Bible, English Standard Version®. ESV® Text Edition: 2016. Copyright © 2001 by Crossway, a publishing ministry of Good News Publishers. The ESV® text has been reproduced in cooperation with and by permission of Good News Publishers. Unauthorised reproduction of this publication is prohibited. All rights reserved.

Scripture quotations marked (NKJV) are taken from the New King James Version®. Copyright © 1982 by Thomas Nelson. Used by permission. All rights reserved.

Scripture quotations marked (TPT) are taken from The Passion Translation®. Copyright © 2017 by BroadStreet Publishing® Group, LLC. Used by permission. All rights reserved. ThePassionTranslation.com.

Scripture quotations marked (ERV) are taken from The Easy-to-Read Version, which is an English translation of the Bible by the World Bible Translation Center (WBTC), a subsidiary of Bible League International. It was originally published as the English Version for the Deaf (EVD) by BakerBooks. Copyright © 2006 by Bible League International.

Scripture quotations marked (CSB) are taken from The Christian Standard Bible. Copyright © 2017 by Holman Bible Publishers. Used by permission. Christian Standard Bible®, and CSB® are federally registered trademarks of Holman Bible Publishers. All rights reserved.

Scripture quotations marked (AKJV) are taken from The Authorized (King James) Version of the Bible ('the KJV'), the rights in which are vested in the Crown in the United Kingdom, is reproduced here by permission of the Crown's patentee, Cambridge University Press.

Scripture quotations marked (BBE) are taken from The Bible in Basic English. The Bible in Basic English was translated by Professor Samuel Henry Hooke (1874-1968), an English scholar and Professor Emeritus of Old Testament Studies at the University of London. The BBE was printed in 1965 by Cambridge Press in England. Published without any copyright notice and distributed in America, this work fell immediately and irretrievably into the public domain in the United States. Copy Freely.

ISBN: 978-0-9929960-2-4

Acknowledgements

Firstly, I would like to acknowledge and thank The Prince of Peace, Jesus Christ, who has taken the time to reveal the possibility of real peace here on Earth. I don't know why He gave me the mandate of sharing this peace with others, but I am grateful that He saw me as worthy, even before I did. I would also like to thank my mother, who has been a constant source of inspiration, reminding me that despite the odds, "I Can". This book wouldn't be complete without thanking my life partner, who consistently reminds me that the pursuit of purpose isn't always plain sailing and encourages me to press on anyway. I would like to acknowledge my children, who push me to be the best version of myself I can be in order to propel them into achieving greater. A special thank you to my sister for being one of the only people I can both laugh and cry with, even in the same conversation. Thank you also to my friends, family and the members of The Rock Church London for supporting me and keeping me grounded.

Much appreciation to Jadanna Lijkendijk for insisting that she draft read this project despite giving birth a few weeks prior. Thank you for being the definition of a true friend. I must also thank Melissa Nankoo for her hard work in draft reading this book and providing valuable feedback. When you find a makeup artist with both vision and therapeutic fingers, you keep her! Thank you Ayo Adegboyega for using your creativity to make a masterpiece of my face. To Dr Adam Ibrahim, Mimi Ajala, Melissa Nankoo and Pastor Ryan A. Johnson, thank you for taking the time out of your busy schedules to walk with me on this journey and provide a compelling quote for the book. To the director of 29Eleven Publishing, my husband, Gbenga Ajewole: Despite your many roles and responsibilities, thank you for always competently handling the important yet often overlooked background duties in order to make our dreams a reality.

Lastly, I would like to thank anyone I have ever worked with in a clinical or pastoral capacity for illuminating the need for a remedy to sorrow and stretching my capacity to create one. An absence of pain is not required for the presence of peace. May your latter be greater than your former, God bless you all always.

Quotes

Selone Ajewole offers the seemingly impossible: a systematic, thoughtful and personal consultation from the pages of her book. She combines technical know-how on CBT and psychotherapy, with, at times painfully personal reflection and insight into our daily struggles. Selone pulls no punches, and her insights will make you feel uncomfortable, but in that safe way only a gifted therapist can. So sit down, avoid distractions, and with prayerful meditation, begin with her a journey to a more peaceful, whole you, you won't regret it.

Dr Adam Ibrahim DipProfDev, BSc, MBBS, DipCBT
Clinical Psychiatrist and former GP Registrar

This book *From Pieces to Peace* is striking in its ability to not only bring clarity on mental health issues that could have confused many Christians but also provides practical solutions to many overlooked yet common emotional and mental health concerns. Pastor Selone has drawn from her wealth of knowledge, bridging the gap between scriptures and everyday challenges faced by individuals from all walks of life. Great and easy read!

Mimi Ajala
Author of "The Life God Has For You: Stop Living Less Than You Are."
Director of Mimi Ajala Ministries

From Pieces to Peace is true to life, and uncovers ways in which you can access peace regardless of your own life story. This book provides warm and wisdom filled insight into a journey that we should all go on. Ultimately, the words on these pages feel a bit like therapy but in book form.

Melissa Nankoo
Pharmacist

From Pieces to Peace: Finding Peace in 5 Key Areas of Your Life captures the steps required to achieve peace from past anxieties. By highlighting how we can often engage in destructive thinking without being aware of it, this book uses scripture and practical psychotherapeutic steps to illustrate how we can combat this Negative Automatic Thinking (NATs) for good. Overall, it helps to start a journey into healthy positive thinking that can alter our spiritual, physical and emotional lives thus helping us to experience peace, pushing us one step closer to achieving our full purpose.

Pastor Ryan A. Johnson
Senior Pastor of Awaken Church

Foreword

As the clay is in the potter's hand, so are you in my hand. (Jeremiah 18:6, NLT)

The words spoken to Prophet Jeremiah, a biblical voice who knew a thing or two about anguish, anxiety and pain, helps us to recognise that we can also trust that our brokenness is fixable. It teaches us that if we choose to anchor ourselves on God, His hands are big enough, loving enough and patient enough to take the broken pieces of our hearts, our relationships and our lives to make us whole again.

Having spent the past eighteen years together, I've had the privileged opportunity to watch the amazing author of this book from the front row (who also happens to be my incredible wife) navigate life and be a cheerleader for peaceful living. Selone has enabled our family and I to cultivate and maintain a state of peace and tranquility in our home over the years, irrespective of all life has had to throw at us.

From Pieces to Peace is a brave book that marries the often-divorced worlds of psychotherapy and faith together in a seamless convergence that will hold the hands of the reader on their journey to encountering internal peace. Selone weaves through and merges her wisdom, years of psychotherapy practice, and her own life experiences to help those who will allow the pages of this book to speak to their soul and find their way to the holy grail of our human existence – peace. My wife spills not only her professional knowledge into this masterpiece of a book, but also removes the veil from her own personal thoughts and life, so that hope can be found, by those seeking it.

From Pieces to Peace, if you allow it to, will speak to your core, whilst helping you to realign both your cognitive disposition and outlook on life, so that you might be able to live out a life that maybe until now, has felt like a distant dream. The five key areas of life (internal, health, relationships, career and finances) that are dealt with in the pages of this book will help kick-start your journey to freedom and wholeness.

This is a book, not just worth reading and sharing with others, but it is a book worth living!

Gbenga Michael Ajewolé
Co-Author, The Colours of Love Relationship Manual
Senior Pastor, The Rock Church London
Proud Husband

Contents

Introduction	1
A Matter of the Mind	9
Autopilot	23
Unexpected Drama	65
Peace Within	79
Health Wise	93
Love in Peace	115
Peace in Purpose	131
Financial Serenity	143
The Invitation	171
References	183
About the Author	187
Notes	189

Introduction

The Pursuit of Peace

"Do you have peace?" That's the question my client, William (pseudonym), asked me during our fourth counselling session together. William was a 28-year-old Finance student, attempting to undertake the second year of his degree again. It seems the anxiety and depression that caused him to drop out one year prior had been festering, and William was concerned. In all my years of practice as a psychotherapist/counsellor, seldom had I been asked such a direct question. Taken aback slightly, my mind flooded with the guidelines and ethical considerations of counselling training. As therapists, we are encouraged to avert such direct questions so to keep the focus on our clients, rather than shifting it onto ourselves. Before I could contain it however, the words "Yes, I do have peace" were boldly ushered out of my mouth.

The tilting of William's head to the side and the slow but steady squinting of his eyes spoke volumes of his desire to know more. Even so, the conversation continued on in a different direction, but I found myself stuck on the notion that peace would in fact be the answer to all of his problems. I began hoping he would ask me where exactly I had found this peace that seemed to so cunningly evade him. Being that many counselling scholars advocate minimal therapist self-disclosure, an internal conflict erupted. Before I had the chance to sufficiently gather my thoughts, almost as though he had been reading my mind without my knowledge or consent, the question "Where do you get this peace from?" was freely flung into the atmosphere. Knowing that an honest answer would have been tinged heavily with religious rather than psychotherapeutic undertones, I gulped inside, feeling like I was beginning to tread in murky waters. Still, being that congruence is one of the core conditions in the therapeutic relationship that helps facilitate healing for the client, I felt it necessary to provide William with transparency in my response (Rogers, 1957). "William, my peace doesn't come from me. I have an anchor, something that doesn't move or shake, even when my world does. *My* peace comes from *my* faith in Jesus Christ. Wherever you find *your* peace, it has to be an unmovable anchor."

After this intense exchange of words, it became apparent that even though most people do not ask as directly as William did, all clients that enter into therapy are desperately seeking one thing: peace. Processing this thought a little deeper, I was able to draw parallels with humanity at large. Although we may not all opt for a course of psychotherapy, in one way or another, we are all searching for peace. Unfortunately, mental distress, emotional turmoil, stressful environments, uncertainty about the future or physical pain will inevitably plague us all at some stage of our lives. Although the cause of this unrest will undoubtedly differ amongst the billions of people on our planet, whether we verbalise it or not, we are all in our own way hoping for the alleviation of symptoms, enabling us to feel at peace within ourselves. Hoping for peace is common practice, but the actual pursuit of peace is something only few will ever engage in. Since you are reading this book, *you* are included in this number.

Good clinical practice in counselling and psychotherapy, amongst many things, requires a real depth of self-reflection. In reflecting on the source of this peace that felt somewhat difficult to articulate with William, something profound illuminated within my being. I began to recognise that even though I am an integrative psychotherapist with a wide array of theories, models, frameworks and practical tools at my disposal, these ideas in and of themselves, although effective, are not enough to help *sustain* lasting peace. For me, cultivating lasting peace within myself, my health, my relationships, my career and my finances (the 5 key areas of this book) has involved a course of making practical changes in both my cognitions and behaviours. However, I believe that the only way I have maintained this state of peace, even when trouble does come knocking, has been by tapping into a source bigger than life itself.

Let's be Specific

In my efforts to appear inclusive or politically correct, the initial drafting of this book had a more generic feel as to what this 'source bigger than life itself' could look like for those who do not subscribe to the Christian faith. The truth is, I really don't know, and as such, it would be unfair for me to comment on it. As I continued to dissect my thoughts and feelings on the matter, I recognised that opting to use the word 'Spirituality' rather than 'Christianity' could not accurately depict the source of lasting peace *I* have personally experienced or witnessed, specifically in most Christian clients. It seems that despite the tumultuous circumstances faced, there appears to be a unique ability amongst many Christians (who focus more on Christ than their problem) to soar peacefully above the storm, like an eagle riding it out, assured of the brighter days ahead. To remove any potential ambiguity that may arise therefore, alongside psychotherapeutic and practical examples and techniques, this book centres on the transformative power of using one's faith in Jesus Christ as a weapon of choice to fight against anything seeking to destroy one's sense of peace. Whether you sing in the choir or avoid religion like the plague, biblical principles are great ones to live by, since the Bible itself focuses heavily on peaceful living here on Earth, as well as in Heaven.

Peace is a Gift

"Peace I leave with you; my peace I give you. I do not give to you as the world gives. Do not let your hearts be troubled and do not be afraid." John 14:27 (NIV)

When a person is about to die, it is common practice for them to leave their possessions to their loved ones by way of a last will and testament. Rather than leaving temporary material goods, just before He died and transcended into heaven, Jesus Christ left something for us all that money couldn't buy: peace! The type of peace that He provides is not predicated on things going right. Peace is often depicted as an expensive Maldives holiday resort advert, where tranquility is assumed to exist only in the secluded brown beach huts surrounded by transparent water, luscious greenery and clear blue skies, which only the rich have access to. On the contrary. What this scripture is saying is that you don't have to wait for the raging tornado that is picking up, twisting round and destroying everything in its wake, to pass, before you can let go of fear and experience peace. There is a peace available to you from God, which *"exceeds anything we can understand"* (Philippians 4:7, NLT). This book will either help introduce you to it or reacquaint you with it.

INTRODUCTION

Mixology: Christianity and Psychotherapy

As fallible human beings living in an imperfect world, unexpected curveballs destined to disrupt our peace will at some stage be thrown through our glass windows of life, with the potential to shatter everything we once held dear. It would be unrealistic to assume that there will not be times where our peace is momentarily knocked off course. The marrying of biblical principles, psychotherapeutic ideology and practical examples and techniques within this book will help you to better manage and recover quicker when this does occur.

This marrying of the Bible and psychotherapy to help combat issues and induce peace, for me, has not been something that has been easy to accomplish. Perhaps this is because this has at some level been counterintuitive to the Black and Christian culture I have grown up in. When I look at this objectively, both have subtly opposed the use of psychotherapy (which is defined as a talking therapy used to treat emotional problems and mental health conditions) in the pursuit of peace. For example, in my experience of growing up within Black culture, coping mechanisms for stress usually constituted having brief conversations *within* the community, as seeking professional help was taboo. It may come as no surprise then that Blacks are overrepresented in the psychiatric system and are less likely to be offered or accept counselling (Brooks, 2009). Similarly, the Christian culture I grew up in referenced scriptures such as Isaiah 9:6 (KJV) in the Bible, where Christ is referred to as the *"wonderful counsellor"*. Seeking counsel from a supernatural God rather than a mortal human when dealing with the pressures of life is so strongly advocated that a number of my Christian clients experience difficulty in acknowledging that they too have succumbed to everyday mental health issues such as anxiety or depression, and are not experiencing peace. This book seeks to make it acceptable in the first instance to admit that 'Christian or not', we all experience moments where we feel anything but peaceful. It then utilises both Christianity and psychotherapy to help move you forward to more peaceful horizons.

In addition, although a study found that only 29% of psychotherapists support the integration of Christianity and psychotherapy, I believe it was a combination of the two that enabled me to release the 11 years of grief I held onto after the murder of my 24-year-old cousin on his doorstep, during a sunny afternoon in March, after going to watch his little sister perform at her school play (Bergin, 1980; Bergin & Jensen, 1990). Alongside the use of my faith, a year-long weekly course of psychotherapy with a stranger helped me to talk about all of those emotions and thoughts I had kept locked away in my private cupboard for years. It is this same grace that we offer to the members of our local community and those who I serve in the dual capacity of pastor and psychotherapist at The Rock Church London. Rather than simply comforting or, at worse, pacifying grieving individuals with scriptures of reuniting with loved ones in Heaven, for example, we also make time to work through *how* they are experiencing this loss now, whilst they are here on Earth. The fusing of relevant biblical promises and examples with psychotherapeutic technique helps me to walk with them at their pace, as they search for peace during our counselling sessions. This is what we will also do together as we work closely throughout this book.

Brighter Days Ahead

If you sit in darkness long enough, you get used to it. As a psychotherapist, my job is to stroll with you while it is dark, as we work together to bring about awareness of *what* may be causing you to leak peace in different areas of your life. The quicker you can identify the source of the leak, the quicker you can attend to the wound and stem the likelihood of any lasting damage being done. When you shine a light in darkness, your eyes may squint at first, but they do eventually adjust, and your future looks brighter because of it.

Like a course of counselling or psychotherapy, the purpose of this book therefore is to encourage you to be more cognizant of and understand better the type of situations that are likely to rob you of peace and cause discomfort in your life. The client and personal stories around everyday struggles with peace help to normalise the fact that we all leak peace from time to time. It will prompt you to look more objectively at the process involved in regaining peace, when it seems to be slipping like grains of sand through one's fingertips. These passages will equip you with the necessary tools to make cognitive and behavioural changes accordingly, opening you up to the endless possibilities of having peace as your default setting, most of the time. You may wish to read this book cover to cover or focus on one of the 5 key areas you are experiencing a lack of peace in, such as within yourself, your health, your relationships, your career or within your finances. Either way, applying these principles will help you experience a sense of calm whilst in the midst of the storm. Remember, as one definition of the word peace suggests, peace is not the absence of worry, but rather a state of being uninterrupted by it. Come; let's go together on your journey, from pieces to peace.

A Matter of the Mind

Christina was a 31-year-old client who had been medically diagnosed with anxiety due to being pre-occupied with worry about how her future would pan out. She thought that the medication prescribed by her doctor would be enough to help eradicate her concerns. A few weeks later however, Christina was mortified to find that when she was faced with unexpected environmental stress, she found herself curled up in that same corner, sweating, crying and shaking, suffering from the familiar symptoms of the panic attacks she was told that her medication would combat. As with many clients with similar presenting issues, it finally became clear to Christina that the medication prescribed could not do all of the work. As we processed this realisation a little deeper, it became apparent that this battle with worry began and ended in her mind, and that the lens through which she looked at life would determine her response.

Worry: The Peace Robber

Peace is defined as: *A state of tranquility or quiet. A freedom from disquieting or oppressive thoughts or emotions.* Christina had succumbed to the disquieting and oppressive thoughts of "What if…", and almost by default, her mind consistently played out the most negative scenarios possible without her even realising it. Believe it or not, many of us find ourselves in a similar state. It is heightened by our existence in such a fast-paced world, prompting us to carry our phones and tablets everywhere with us, including into our once sacred and serene bath time by way of a waterproof phone case. It is no wonder then that *we seldom think about what we are actually thinking about*, and this is how worry sets in.

I heard a story recently of a pastor describing the best way to cook a frog. Now, although many of us may not willingly choose to season and devour this type of four-legged creature, the sentiments of the story are profound enough to wake us up like an over-zealous alarm clock. The frog is to be placed inside a large pot that it can't get out of without jumping extremely high. If the heat is turned up slowly enough, in small increments, the frog will remain blissfully unaware that it is being cooked, until it is too late to do anything about it. The same is true of worry. Little by little, it heats you up, making your blood boil, until you find yourself drained of all life. You see, the frog has an innate ability, unlike many other creatures, to jump high enough to remove itself from the danger. However, its lack of awareness of this worsening situation will unfortunately require payment of a very hefty price. Could you be in a more serious state of worry than you are aware of?

The definition of worry is: *To feel or cause to feel anxious or troubled about actual or potential problems.* The latter part of this definition suggests that worry is persuasive enough to encourage you to expel precious energy on something that *may never even happen*. Where are you with that? Antonyms for peace include unrest, anxiety, turmoil, disharmony, frustration, distress and, unsurprisingly, worry. Peace and worry are on opposing teams; before we go any further in this book, you will need to choose which team you are on.

Guard Your Mind

Cognitive Behavioural psychologists have long highlighted the great impact our cognitions (thoughts) have on our subsequent behaviours (Beck, 1967; Ellis, 1957, 1962). If you don't take a moment to bring what you are thinking about into consciousness, all of these negative adjectives will continue to rear their ugly heads automatically and without any opposition. This is known as Negative Automatic Thinking (NATs), which many of us suffer from without even realising it (Beck, 1976). These types of negative thoughts are automatic and require no effort on our part; they simply pop into our minds and take root. They often start small and might be as simple as, "I'm always getting things wrong", or, "This is going to be a bad day", or, "There is no way I can solve this problem, my life is doomed to failure." The impact of allowing negative automatic thinking to rule your mind can be more destructive than you know. Without being aware of these thoughts, there is no way to challenge them as distorted and unhelpful. This is perhaps why Proverbs 4:23 (CEV) forewarns: *"Carefully guard your thoughts because they are the source of true life."*

Although it may be uncomfortable lifting the lid on the complexities of our unconscious thought processing, the popular phrase 'Knowledge is power' is definitely applicable here. The more aware we are of our thinking, the more conscious we become of how much we are leaving the door ajar for negative thoughts and emotions to reproduce and further disillusion us. This will in turn determine how much these thoughts become the lens through which we look at life and, ultimately, how peaceful a life we lead. Perception is key! In counselling sessions, I have noticed how two people can go through very similar circumstances yet choose entirely different responses based only on their perception. Two individuals could unexpectedly step in dog poo and one may blame themselves for being clumsy and unfocused, whilst the other may simply shrug and state that "Shit happens". Which one of these best describes you? Becoming conscious of your thinking and training your responses when not in times of crisis will better enable your default response to either a major or minor unexpected event to not be blown out of proportion, and to affiliate more closely with peace than panic.

Negative Automatic Thinking Illumination

There are several different kinds of negative thoughts that may occupy your mind and, in turn, cause you to worry. These thoughts can be imperceptible and, for the most part, float around in our minds unnoticed and without reprimand. Listed below are five examples of NATs, but further research should increase your knowledge on what to look out for.

Personalising: These are thoughts that encourage the belief that something is either your fault or that the thoughts and behaviours of others are undertaken in reaction to you.

Example: "Harry seems really cross; I must have done something to upset him."

Overgeneralisation: These types of thoughts involve drawing general conclusions, despite the lack of evidence to support the claim. The words "always" and "never" often feature.

Example: "I missed the deadline again. I will NEVER be good at this."

Dichotomous Reasoning: This involves a tendency to view things in extremes rather than on different scales of the spectrum (i.e. good or bad, right or wrong).

Example: "This report is so bad; there is nothing good about it."

Catastrophising: These types of thoughts include overestimated assumptions of disaster.

Example: "I think I left the flat iron on, the house will burn down."

Selective Abstraction: This type of thinking centres on filtering important information to support a negative viewpoint.

Example: "My lecturer said my essay was excellent but there were a few errors to correct. He must think I am really stupid."

Negative Automatic Thinking: Exercise One

None of us is exempt from experiencing negative automatic thinking from time to time. Can you identify yourself in any of the types of thinking listed above? If so, please outline any examples of those you have experienced.

_____
_____
_____
_____

If you have been able to identify yourself in any of these thoughts, how does it feel to acknowledge this?

_____
_____
_____
_____

Overall, what kind of thoughts occupy your thinking most of the time?

_____
_____
_____
_____

In an average day, how much of your thoughts appear to have a negative undertone?

_____ %

In an average day, how much of your thoughts appear to have a positive undertone?

_____ %

How do you feel about the ratio above?

What impact do you believe this has on your state of peace at the moment?

What long-term future impact do you believe it may have if it remains as is?

Living in a world where bad news occupies news stations globally more than good news, it would perhaps be unrealistic to think that we could maintain positive thoughts every moment of every day. If however you could shift the ratio above, what percentages would you assign to the types of thoughts you are thinking every day?

____ % Positive Thoughts

____ % Negative Thoughts

Combatting Negative Automatic Thinking

Your participation in the exercise above may have allowed you to identify elements of negative automatic thinking in your own life. The next part of this chapter will provide you with the necessary tools to combat or at least lessen the frequency of these types of thoughts. If negative automatic thinking has been ingrained within you for some time however, it may take some time to undo. My clinical work has demonstrated that with an unwavering commitment to freeing up one's mind with space to dream of better, it is possible to re-train one's thinking to be more in line with thoughts that on the whole induce more peace and positivity and less worry and negativity.

Writing down your negative automatic thoughts as soon as they occur is an important part of the strategy required to overcome them, as outlined by Beck (1976). Because this may not always be possible in the moment, perhaps setting some time aside to do this in the evening could be used as an alternative.

Negative Automatic Thinking: Exercise Two

Write down:

A: Describe a situation you were in which evoked various thoughts and emotions.

_____

_____

_____

_____

B: What were your thoughts?

_____

_____

_____

_____

C: What were your subsequent feelings and behaviour?

_____

_____

_____

_____

Were any of your thoughts and beliefs about (A) negative and automatic? If so, outline them.

_____
_____
_____
_____

Could any of your thoughts about (A) have been influenced by a previous situation? If so, please outline this.

_____
_____
_____
_____

Next, dispute these negative and automatic thoughts. What other ways of thinking could you have engaged in?

_____
_____
_____
_____

How would these alternative or perhaps more rational thoughts have affected the emotions and behaviours experienced at (C)?

_____

_____

_____

_____

If in future a similar situation should arise, what learning could you apply and what might be the outcome?

_____

_____

_____

_____

Taking time out to become more aware of the negative automatic thinking experienced will put you in a good position to resist them.

That Sinking Feeling

Boats don't sink because they went inside water, they sink because they let the water get into them. Even in the midst of a tumultuous storm, Jesus Himself demonstrated to us that we can have peace (Mark 4: 38-40, NIV). Though the waves were tossing the boat to and fro during a raging storm, Jesus Christ was found sleeping peacefully, confusing and annoying those around Him because His first response pertained to peace, rather than worry, panic or fear. He understood that He was responsible for choosing how to respond to this unexpected crisis. Furthermore, He recognised that to choose worry during this catastrophe would be counterproductive, as it does not solve the situation and definitely does not induce peace. Jesus was clear that we cannot make good decisions or problem solve effectively if we allow our minds to be consumed with chaos. Perhaps this is why Philippians 4:6 (GW) reminds us *"Never worry about anything. But in every situation, let God know what you need in prayers and requests while giving thanks."* If we so desire it, *"the Lord of peace himself"* can and will *"give you his peace at all times and in every situation"* (2 Thessalonians 3:16, NLT). This scripture is reminding us that we can have peace, no matter the circumstance, because God's peace resists the atmosphere of this world. "How do you receive this peace?" I hear you ask. God has created a special place of calm where we can meet Him in simple and honest communication (prayer), where you are honest about the uncertainty you feel but you don't give in to your situation. This special place does not need to be a physical location, but rather, it can be somewhere you travel to in your mind. This place is available to us all; you just have to allow yourself to be led there. It simply involves striking up a conversation with God in your mind or aloud, like you would a friend or a loving father.

Whenever you feel worried, instead of heightening your sense of anxiety with the "What ifs…" by either reading negative reports online, speaking to negative people or conjuring up negative thoughts in your own mind, you can read Matthew 6:34 (MSG), which advises: *"Give your entire attention to what God is doing right now, and don't get worked up about what may or may not happen tomorrow. God will help you deal with whatever hard things come up when the time comes."* I am still learning however, that it is not enough to just read this or similar scriptures. I have to believe it, write it on a Post-it note or type it into my phone, look at it, learn it, and recite it when feeling shaky. In time, this scripture became the gate at which I allowed or stopped certain thoughts from taking root in my mind. Why not Google biblical scriptures on peace and note down your favourite ones on your phone or in your journal? For those of you who are new or alien to Christianity, The Message Bible or New Living Translation versions may be easiest to understand in the first instance. The mind is more powerful than we give it credit. Whatever you allow to take root in your mind will grow. This is why Isaiah 26:3-4 (MSG) reminds us to focus our mind on God. It reads: *"People with their minds set on you, you keep completely whole, steady on their feet, because they keep at it and don't quit. Depend on God and keep at it because in the Lord God, you have a sure thing."* If we do this, we can be sure that lasting peace will begin to flourish.

A Daily Renewal of the Mind

So, this peace described above is yours for the taking, if you choose to receive it. Let's be clear however, if negative thinking and worry has plagued your existence for the majority of your life, positive thinking and peace is unlikely to replace your way of being overnight. Whenever you are trying to swim against the current, it will require you to fight. You have to decide to store up the energy you normally ascribe to worry and change its usage. True transformation will require a daily renewal of your mind (Romans 12:2, NIV). You will need to remind yourself on a daily basis of the *new you* that you are becoming. Will you have moments of relapse? Being that we are all in fact imperfect human beings, this is highly likely. How quickly you identify that you have stumbled and get back onto your journey after a trip or fall, however, will be key to sustaining your newly found serenity.

Autopilot

So far, we have established that although peace is something many desire, only few will ever wholeheartedly pursue it. We have also explored the view that our battle for peace begins in our mind and that our cognitions play a major role in ensuring victory. Since cognitions affect behaviours and we have already begun lifting the lid on their impact, it is equally imperative for us to analyse our behaviours and lifestyle practices. If we do not have these in check, it will be futile to seek to develop and sustain peace in those five key areas of our lives: peace within, in our health, relationships, finances and our careers. Taking inventory of our daily routine and how much room there is for peace to operate is vital to moving forward and making a change for the better. This of course is easier said than done however, since most of our daily routine is conducted whilst in a state of 'autopilot'. Human beings across the world spend much of their day 'doing', without thinking or being present in the moment. This chapter seeks to highlight what we are thinking and feeling in the midst of the 'doing', outlining exactly where we can make changes to increase our sense of peace.

Mindfulness

Mindfulness is defined as: The psychological process of bringing one's attention to experiences occurring in the present moment, which can be developed through the practice of meditation and other training (Mindfulness). Although mindfulness stems from Buddhist tradition, Clinical psychology and psychiatry research has demonstrated a strong correlation between therapeutic variants of mindfulness and greater mental wellbeing (Baer et al., 2008; Bränström, Duncan, Moskowitz & Tedlie, 2011). Furthermore, mindfulness is also associated with the reduction of worry and rumination, which are known to heighten anxiety and depression (Creswell, 2017; Gu, Strauss, Bond & Cavanagh, 2015; Querstret & Cropley, 2013). Using mindfulness therefore can help to develop self-knowledge and wisdom, which eventually leads to enlightenment about how best to make modifications to benefit one's future. Before we delve into the practicalities of mindfulness and how incorporating your own version of it may assist in your pursuit of peace, it's important to take a frank look at how peaceful your day to day living is and identify places where we can make healthier alterations.

Shortly you will be asked to map out your average weekday routine. An example has been done for you.

My Average Weekday Routine Example

5:00am

Activity: Sleeping

Thought:

Feeling: Anxious   Frustrated   Worried   Relaxed

Balanced   Peaceful   Other: _____

6:00am

Activity: Sleeping

Thought:

Feeling: Anxious   Frustrated   Worried   Relaxed

             Balanced   Peaceful   Other: _____

7:00am

Activity: Wake up, pray/read Bible, check social media, 20 minutes exercise

Thought: Hurry up; you are going to be late again!

Feeling: **Anxious** Frustrated   Worried   Relaxed

             Balanced   Peaceful   Other: _____

8:00am

Activity: Shower, breakfast, get children ready, school run, drive to work

Thought: Why can't these kids listen the first time! I hope there is no traffic.

Feeling: Anxious **Frustrated** Worried Relaxed

Balanced Peaceful Other: _____

9:00am

Activity: Arrive at work, attend briefing, prioritise workload, talk to colleagues

Thought: This is going to be a long day!

Feeling: **Anxious** Frustrated Worried Relaxed

Balanced Peaceful Other: _____

10:00am

Activity: Begin working on report, answering phone calls, drinking coffee

Thought: Pace yourself, you can manage, you should be finished by 11:00am

Feeling: Anxious   Frustrated   Worried   Relaxed

Balanced   Peaceful   Other: _____

11:00am

Activity: Still working on report, attended emergency meeting

Thought: I should be finished this report by now!

Feeling: Anxious   **Frustrated**   Worried   Relaxed

Balanced   Peaceful   Other: _____

12:00pm

Activity: Lunchtime: Still working on report, checking social media, quick chat with hubby

Thought: I have to get this report finished, no time for a real break.

Feeling: Anxious   Frustrated   Worried   Relaxed

Balanced   Peaceful   **Other: Irritated**

1:00pm

Activity: Client meeting, intense negotiations

Thought: This is what I'm good at

Feeling: Anxious   Frustrated   Worried   Relaxed

Balanced   Peaceful   **Other: Confident**

2:00pm

Activity: Typing up terms agreed with client, taking phone calls, responding to emails

Thought: When is it home time?

Feeling: Anxious   Frustrated   Worried   Relaxed

                Balanced   Peaceful   **Other: Lethargic**

3:00pm

Activity: 5-minute fresh air break, check social media, continuing working

Thought: I need a quick break.

Feeling: Anxious   Frustrated   Worried   Relaxed

                Balanced   Peaceful   **Other: Refreshed**

4:00pm

Activity: Tidying desk, noting down priorities for tomorrow, finishing emails

Thought: Can't wait to finish. Will there be traffic when I get the kids? There's lots to do when I get home, I just want to relax.

Feeling: **Anxious** Frustrated Worried Relaxed

Balanced Peaceful Other: _____

5:00pm

Activity: Left work at 4:59pm, saw boss on the way down, gave me a funny look

Thought: Will I be in trouble tomorrow?

Feeling: Anxious Frustrated **Worried** Relaxed

Balanced Peaceful Other: _____

6:00pm

Activity: The children and I are home, prepare a snack for them, start homework, begin getting dinner ready

Thought: Roll on bedtime for me and the kids!

Feeling: Anxious   Frustrated   Worried   Relaxed

              Balanced   Peaceful   **Other: Tired**

7:00pm

Activity: Eat with family, get children ready for bed, read bedtime story

Thought: I really wish I had more of me to give to the children by the end of the day, they do make me laugh.

Feeling: Anxious   **Frustrated**   Worried   Relaxed

              Balanced   Peaceful   Other: _____

8:00pm

Activity: Clean up the kitchen, neaten kids' room, chat and laugh with hubby, put clothes to wash

Thought: Yay! Us time!

Feeling: Anxious   Frustrated   Worried   **Relaxed**

Balanced   Peaceful   Other: _____

9:00pm

Activity: Watch our favourite TV programme, eat some salted caramel chocolate

Thought: Enjoying chilling with hubby, but need to get to bed soon!

Feeling: Anxious   Frustrated   Worried   Relaxed

Balanced   **Peaceful**   Other: _____

10:00pm

Activity: Pray, check social media, internet searches

Thought: Getting really tired now.

Feeling: Anxious   Frustrated   Worried   Relaxed

Balanced   Peaceful   **Other: Shattered**

11:00pm

Activity: Fall asleep

Thought:

Feeling: Anxious   Frustrated   Worried   Relaxed

Balanced   **Peaceful**   Other: _____

12:00am

Activity: Sleep

Thought:

Feeling: Anxious   Frustrated   Worried   Relaxed

Balanced   Peaceful   Other: _____

1:00am

Activity: Get up to soothe our 3-year-old child who has just woken from a nightmare

Thought: Mummy loves you baby but I'm tired!!

Feeling: Anxious   **Frustrated**   Worried   Relaxed

               Balanced   Peaceful   Other: _____

2:00am

Activity: Can't get back to sleep, scroll through social media

Thought: Tomorrow is going to be a long day!

Feeling: **Anxious**   Frustrated   Worried   Relaxed

               Balanced   Peaceful   Other: _____

3:00am

Activity: Fell asleep again

Thought: This is going to be a long day!

Feeling: **Anxious**   Frustrated   Worried   Relaxed

               Balanced   Peaceful   Other: _____

4:00am

Activity: Sleep

Thought:

Feeling: Anxious   Frustrated   Worried   Relaxed

Balanced   Peaceful   Other: _____

In this example, much of the day is filled with tasks undertaken at work, which sometimes involve meeting unattainable deadlines. Breaks are spent checking social media or searching the internet, as is the case for many individuals in present day society. In addition, when exploring the thought behind the activity, we recognise that this in turn produces a 'feeling'. In this scenario, the majority of the feelings during the day did not pertain to peace. The most dangerous part of this however is that since most of our day is undertaken whilst on autopilot, a lot of what we are thinking and feeling goes unnoticed and therefore builds up, decreasing the likelihood of us ever experiencing a felt sense of peace. Whilst we may not all enjoy our present circumstances in terms of work or study, we can still find moments of fulfilment. Examining the thoughts and feelings behind everyday activities you carry out will help to shed some light on exactly how peaceful the smaller moments in your day are, which impacts how serene a life you are leading overall. What does an average weekday look like for you? Perhaps choose a recent weekday that you could explore in depth.

Map out your average *weekday* routine. Feel free to circle more than one feeling where applicable.

5:00am

Activity: _____

Thought: _____

Feeling: Anxious   Frustrated   Worried   Relaxed

            Balanced   Peaceful   Other: _____

6:00am

Activity: _____

Thought: _____

Feeling: Anxious   Frustrated   Worried   Relaxed

            Balanced   Peaceful   Other: _____

AUTOPILOT

7:00am

Activity: _____

Thought: _____

Feeling: Anxious   Frustrated   Worried   Relaxed

   Balanced   Peaceful   Other: _____

8:00am

Activity: _____

Thought: _____

Feeling: Anxious   Frustrated   Worried   Relaxed

   Balanced   Peaceful   Other: _____

9:00am

Activity: _____

Thought: _____

Feeling: Anxious   Frustrated   Worried   Relaxed

   Balanced   Peaceful   Other: _____

10:00am

Activity: _____

Thought: _____

Feeling: Anxious   Frustrated   Worried   Relaxed

  Balanced   Peaceful   Other: _____

11:00am

Activity: _____

Thought: _____

Feeling: Anxious   Frustrated   Worried   Relaxed

  Balanced   Peaceful   Other: _____

12:00pm

Activity: _____

Thought: _____

Feeling: Anxious   Frustrated   Worried   Relaxed

  Balanced   Peaceful   Other: _____

1:00pm

Activity: _____

Thought: _____

Feeling: Anxious   Frustrated   Worried   Relaxed

   Balanced   Peaceful   Other: _____

2:00pm

Activity: _____

Thought: _____

Feeling: Anxious   Frustrated   Worried   Relaxed

   Balanced   Peaceful   Other: _____

3:00pm

Activity: _____

Thought: _____

Feeling: Anxious   Frustrated   Worried   Relaxed

   Balanced   Peaceful   Other: _____

4:00pm

Activity: _____

Thought: _____

Feeling: Anxious   Frustrated   Worried   Relaxed

Balanced   Peaceful   Other: _____

5:00pm

Activity: _____

Thought: _____

Feeling: Anxious   Frustrated   Worried   Relaxed

Balanced   Peaceful   Other: _____

6:00pm

Activity: _____

Thought: _____

Feeling: Anxious   Frustrated   Worried   Relaxed

Balanced   Peaceful   Other: _____

AUTOPILOT

7:00pm

Activity: _____

Thought: _____

Feeling: Anxious   Frustrated   Worried   Relaxed

Balanced   Peaceful   Other: _____

8:00pm

Activity: _____

Thought: _____

Feeling: Anxious   Frustrated   Worried   Relaxed

Balanced   Peaceful   Other: _____

9:00pm

Activity: _____

Thought: _____

Feeling: Anxious   Frustrated   Worried   Relaxed

Balanced   Peaceful   Other: _____

10:00pm

Activity: _____

Thought: _____

Feeling: Anxious   Frustrated   Worried   Relaxed

            Balanced   Peaceful   Other: _____

11:00pm

Activity: _____

Thought: _____

Feeling: Anxious   Frustrated   Worried   Relaxed

            Balanced   Peaceful   Other: _____

12:00am

Activity: _____

Thought: _____

Feeling: Anxious   Frustrated   Worried   Relaxed

            Balanced   Peaceful   Other: _____

1:00am

Activity: _____

Thought: _____

Feeling: Anxious   Frustrated   Worried   Relaxed

Balanced   Peaceful   Other: _____

2:00am

Activity: _____

Thought: _____

Feeling: Anxious   Frustrated   Worried   Relaxed

Balanced   Peaceful   Other: _____

3:00am

Activity: _____

Thought: _____

Feeling: Anxious   Frustrated   Worried   Relaxed

Balanced   Peaceful   Other: _____

4:00am

Activity: _____

Thought: _____

Feeling: Anxious   Frustrated   Worried   Relaxed

Balanced   Peaceful   Other: _____

In terms of the 'feeling' behind the activity, what percentage of your day is spent feeling:

Anxious: _____%

Frustrated: _____%

Worried: _____%

Relaxed: _____%

Balanced: _____%

Peaceful: _____%

Other: _____ _____%

Other: _____ _____%

Other: _____ _____%

Have negative feelings been building inside of you? If so, how aware were you that these feelings have been accumulating?

_____
_____
_____
_____

Looking at an average weekday, what percentage of your day is spent:

Exercising: _____%

Prayer/Bible reading, spiritual meditation: _____%

Nature walks: _____%

Conversations with friends: _____%

Laughter: _____%

Working: _____%

Social media/internet surfing: _____%

Watching TV: _____%

Socialising with friends: _____%

Interacting with children: _____%

Attending kids clubs: _____%

Cooking and cleaning: _____%

Intimate moments with spouse: _____%

Family activities: _____%

Personal development: _____%

Date nights: _____%

Reading a book: _____%

Goal setting: _____%

Executing goals: _____%

Financial budgeting: _____%

Academic advancement: _____%

Attempting something new: _____%

Beauty regimen: _____%

'Me time': _____%

Pausing and thinking: _____%

Other: _____ _____%

We all have the power to begin making changes to our daily routine to induce a felt sense of peace, but this first begins with a thought. No thought is too outlandish to put out there into the atmosphere. The Bible says that if we speak or *"decree a thing"*, we can be sure that *"it shall be established"*

(Job 22:28, KJV). To bring about awareness of what it is you truly desire, ask yourself the following questions:

In terms of peace, what is it you dream an average weekday could look like for you and why?

_____

_____

_____

_____

Your answer to the previous question may of course take some time to accomplish. In the meantime, what does a peaceful moment look like to you?

_____

_____

_____

_____

In time, more peaceful moments accumulate to produce a more peaceful day. What modifications are required to help increase the number of peaceful moments you experience in a day?

_____
_____
_____
_____

Cultivating moments of peace in day to day living when you are not facing a crisis can go some way in improving your overall health and state of mind. Name one thing could you eliminate in an average day that tends to rob you of your peace (e.g. communication issues with your partner, dwelling on the past, being unorganised and in a rush every day).

_____
_____
_____
_____

What spiritual or practical tools do you have at your disposal on an average day that you could employ to help evoke a sense of calm?

_____
_____
_____
_____

Name one thing you could incorporate into an average day that helps generate a sense of peace, if only for a moment (e.g. an early morning walk or run outside in nature, a relaxing bath at night time, time set aside for you and your partner to laugh and chill out).

_____
_____
_____
_____

What you surround yourself with is what you become like. On balance, do you surround yourself with more peaceful and positive people or the opposite (e.g. peaceful promises in Bible scriptures, calm and collected friends and family, a tranquil home environment vs. no spiritual nourishment, negative social network, and a stressful and combative home environment)?

_____
_____
_____
_____

'The early bird catches the worm' is a very common yet extremely powerful statement. What else could you accomplish if you were to sleep and wake up earlier (e.g. working on a book, cooking dinner now whilst everyone is asleep to have more time with them in the evening etc.)?

_____
_____
_____
_____

Time is a more precious commodity than many of us realise. Where is most of your time being wasted?

_____
_____
_____
_____

Have you set any goals to help push you towards a more peaceful and fulfilling future (e.g. setting up my own cake baking business etc.)? If not, why not brainstorm some ideas?

_____
_____
_____
_____

It's the weekend!

We should all love that 'Friday feeling' and embrace the approaching weekend but we don't always maximise our time off in the way we should. The hope is that your weekends allow for a little more balance. However, without realising it, many people treat their so-called rest time in the same way that they treat their weekday – in a rush and in a panic. By the same token, others may do absolutely nothing but wallow until Monday comes round again. Having at least one day per week where you relax and enjoy life goes a long way in the recalibration of the soul. Let's explore in detail your current weekend routine and consider any changes required to induce more serenity.

Map out your average *weekend* routine

5:00am

Activity: _____

Thought: _____

Feeling: Anxious   Frustrated   Worried   Relaxed

             Balanced   Peaceful   Other: _____

6:00am

Activity: _____

Thought: _____

Feeling: Anxious   Frustrated   Worried   Relaxed

Balanced   Peaceful   Other: _____

7:00am

Activity: _____

Thought: _____

Feeling: Anxious   Frustrated   Worried   Relaxed

Balanced   Peaceful   Other: _____

8:00am

Activity: _____

Thought: _____

Feeling: Anxious   Frustrated   Worried   Relaxed

Balanced   Peaceful   Other: _____

AUTOPILOT

9:00am

Activity: _____

Thought: _____

Feeling: Anxious   Frustrated   Worried   Relaxed

Balanced   Peaceful   Other: _____

10:00am

Activity: _____

Thought: _____

Feeling: Anxious   Frustrated   Worried   Relaxed

Balanced   Peaceful   Other: _____

11:00am

Activity: _____

Thought: _____

Feeling: Anxious   Frustrated   Worried   Relaxed

Balanced   Peaceful   Other: _____

12:00pm

Activity: _____

Thought: _____

Feeling: Anxious   Frustrated   Worried   Relaxed

Balanced   Peaceful   Other: _____

1:00pm

Activity: _____

Thought: _____

Feeling: Anxious   Frustrated   Worried   Relaxed

Balanced   Peaceful   Other: _____

2:00pm

Activity: _____

Thought: _____

Feeling: Anxious   Frustrated   Worried   Relaxed

Balanced   Peaceful   Other: _____

AUTOPILOT

3:00pm

Activity: _____

Thought: _____

Feeling: Anxious   Frustrated   Worried   Relaxed

Balanced   Peaceful   Other: _____

4:00pm

Activity: _____

Thought: _____

Feeling: Anxious   Frustrated   Worried   Relaxed

Balanced   Peaceful   Other: _____

5:00pm

Activity: _____

Thought: _____

Feeling: Anxious   Frustrated   Worried   Relaxed

Balanced   Peaceful   Other: _____

6:00pm

Activity: _____

Thought: _____

Feeling: Anxious   Frustrated   Worried   Relaxed

Balanced   Peaceful   Other: _____

7:00pm

Activity: _____

Thought: _____

Feeling: Anxious   Frustrated   Worried   Relaxed

Balanced   Peaceful   Other: _____

8:00pm

Activity: _____

Thought: _____

Feeling: Anxious   Frustrated   Worried   Relaxed

Balanced   Peaceful   Other: _____

9:00pm

Activity: _____

Thought: _____

Feeling: Anxious   Frustrated   Worried   Relaxed

　　　　　　Balanced   Peaceful   Other: _____

10:00pm

Activity: _____

Thought: _____

Feeling: Anxious   Frustrated   Worried   Relaxed

　　　　　　Balanced   Peaceful   Other: _____

11:00pm

Activity: _____

Thought: _____

Feeling: Anxious   Frustrated   Worried   Relaxed

　　　　　　Balanced   Peaceful   Other: _____

12:00am

Activity: _____

Thought: _____

Feeling: Anxious   Frustrated   Worried   Relaxed

               Balanced   Peaceful   Other: _____

1:00am

Activity: _____

Thought: _____

Feeling: Anxious   Frustrated   Worried   Relaxed

               Balanced   Peaceful   Other: _____

2:00am

Activity: _____

Thought: _____

Feeling: Anxious   Frustrated   Worried   Relaxed

               Balanced   Peaceful   Other: _____

3:00am

Activity: _____

Thought: _____

Feeling: Anxious   Frustrated   Worried   Relaxed

           Balanced   Peaceful   Other: _____

4:00am

Activity: _____

Thought: _____

Feeling: Anxious   Frustrated   Worried   Relaxed

           Balanced   Peaceful   Other: _____

In terms of the 'feeling' behind the activity, what percentage of your day is spent feeling:

Anxious: _____%

Frustrated: _____%

Worried: _____%

Relaxed: _____%

Balanced: _____%

Peaceful: _____%

Other: _____ _____%

Other: _____ _____%

Other: _____ _____%

Have negative feelings been building inside of you? If so, how aware were you that these feelings have been accumulating?

_____
_____
_____
_____

Looking at an average weekend, what percentage of your day is spent:

Exercising: _____%

Prayer/Bible reading, spiritual meditation: _____%

Nature walks: _____%

Conversations with friends: _____%

Laughter: _____%

Working: _____%

Social media/internet surfing: _____%

Watching TV: _____%

Socialising with friends: _____%

Interacting with children: _____%

Attending kids clubs: _____%

Cooking and cleaning: _____%

Intimate moments with spouse: _____%

Family activities: _____%

Personal development: _____%

Date nights: _____%

Reading a book: _____%

Goal setting: _____%

Executing goals: _____%

Financial budgeting: _____%

Academic advancement: _____%

Attempting something new: _____%

Beauty regimen: _____%

'Me time':   _____%

Pausing and thinking: _____%

Other: _____   _____%

What kind of changes may you need to make to encourage more fulfilment and relaxation in your weekends?

_____
_____
_____
_____

Mindfulness in Action

To achieve greater balance throughout our daily routine, we must become more aware of the impact operating in autopilot mode has on the smaller increments of our day. In the examples above, we have reflected on your thoughts and feelings *after* they have occurred. Mindfulness simply involves paying attention to these thoughts and feelings whilst they are in operation, which can help you to understand yourself better and, in turn, help you to enjoy life more. Moreover, incorporating mindfulness practices 'in the moment' will further enable you to be aware of the happenings inside and outside of your mind and body that are driving your emotions and subsequent behaviours (Williams, 2016). This type of awareness also enables us to recognise signs of the onset of anxiety and depression, empowering us to take action and manage it sooner.

Practicing mindfulness at its most basic level involves (Williams, 2016):

- Noticing everyday things such as the fresh air against our bodies, the tastes and smells of the food we eat, the things that make us laugh or experience a sense of joy. Paying attention to the small things goes a long way in interrupting the autopilot mode we often engage in.
- Picking a regular time every day to pause and notice these things will help develop consistency.
- Trying something new like a new venue at lunchtime or walking a different route in your 5-minute nature walk may help give you a fresh perspective on life.
- Trying to watch your thoughts. This might be easier in mediation or whilst engaging in prayer with Jesus Christ early in the morning, or if you can head to a peaceful place for 5 minutes throughout your day. You can name the thoughts, for example, the thought: "I think I will probably fail this assignment" should be named for what it is, e.g.: "This is anxiety."

Although I do endorse mindfulness practice in the pursuit of peace, I believe that engaging in mindfulness without the assistance and assurances of Jesus Christ is counterproductive. This is because without Christ, all the thoughts, both positive and negative, that have illuminated in your being, you then have to carry and cope with all by yourself. With Christ however, any thoughts or feelings about the present, past or future you don't like, you can simply hand over to Him, as Psalm 55:22 (NLT) states: *"Give your burdens to the Lord, and He will take care of you. He will not permit the godly to slip and fall."*

With determination and consistency, mindfulness should increase, autopilot should decrease, and these small changes will become second nature, helping you to better navigate an average day a little more peacefully.

Unexpected Drama

Throughout this book, so far, we have inspected your daily routines in great detail and have explored how your thoughts behind the tasks undertaken on 'autopilot' affect how peaceful you feel. Outside of the norm of our day to day living, it is inevitable that we will be faced with some type of difficulty or crisis, just when we least expect it. Yes, unexpected drama often has a way of arising at the most inopportune times. I was faced with some 'unexpected drama' recently, and truth be told, I found myself struggling to hold onto peace. In simultaneously drafting the pages of this book on peace, I began to feel somewhat hypocritical in my struggle to maintain a sense of tranquility. I decided however that this would be the perfect opportunity to double as a researcher and participant, highlighting any learning that may benefit my readers. The situation unfolded as described below.

A Christmas Surprise

It was a few days before Christmas and I drove to our sons' primary school to pick them up for 1:30pm, since it was the last day of term. I recognised beforehand that the road would be unusually packed, since all of the schoolchildren would be let out at the same time, rather than within the usual 10-minute interval. As I drove up the side road towards the school, I noticed a stream of cars stuck in the middle, unable to move because of a stationary rubbish truck attempting to collect the weekly rubbish from the street. As I looked to my left, I noticed a car parking space big enough for our brand new 4X4 to fit into. As I parked my car in this different location to my usual space, I remember something inside saying to me "Is this a good idea?" However, time was pressed, traffic wasn't moving, and there were no other parking spaces in sight, so I ignored it, hopped out of the car and went to pick up our two boys from their respective classes.

As I walked out of the school with them, they were excited to be heading home, playing tag with their friends for just one last time. I began thinking about where I had parked the car, and the fact that we would most likely need to wait for all the traffic to clear before we would be able to move and turn the car around. As I turned the corner, with my children holding both of my hands, I noticed a large crowd of people around my car, a red and white Christmas present sitting on the bonnet, and a lady in a Ford Fiesta stuck on the side of my monster truck. As I got closer, it felt like time began to stand still. I found myself wondering whether or not she had hit my car slowly disappear, as my eyes confirmed that a man was trying to help her reverse well enough to get off of the side of my vehicle that she had just crashed into. As she moved back, I noticed the damage to the front right bumper, and the man in question stroked it to examine just how bad it was, unaware that I, as the owner, was approaching him. As I calmly stated that it was 'my car', he promptly removed the Christmas present from the bonnet and began to explain that she had hit it by mistake. She said that she would park her car and that she would be over to speak to me in a moment.

Just to put this into context, at least 3 times a week, I witness parents swearing at each other on the verge of physical altercations because of the difficulties in manoeuvring up and down this tight and busy road. The crowd was ready for another fight, but *I* was not going to give it to them. I calmly asked my children to get into the car, took down the details of the witness, and went over to speak to, in my mind, 'the perpetrator of the crime'. For the purposes of this story, we will refer to this lady as 'Lisa'. With makeup running down her face and tears in her eyes, Lisa apologised profusely, maintaining that she was at fault and took full responsibility for the consequences. She mentioned that the "meltdown" she was having caused her to misjudge the situation and to pull in too early, even though there was at least 10 metres of available space. Here I was, staring at our brand new car, scuffed and damaged, yet all I could think to do was to maintain my composure and to check that Lisa and her children were ok, even giving her a hug to help soothe her distress. She was very grateful that I had been so gracious to her. She told me her children's names and that they attended the same school as my sons, and that she wouldn't try to "scam me", giving me all her details and exclaiming that she would of course pay for any damage. Lisa then proceeded to plead with me not to go through the insurance, and explained that her partner was a mechanic. I politely told her that the car would need to be fixed at the dealership we bought it from, and she attested to the fact that this was a more than reasonable request. I took the relevant photos, told her I would be in touch once I had a quote that evening, and wished her and her family a very merry Christmas.

During the whole scenario, on the outside, I appeared calm and peaceful, but on the inside, I was shaking and felt anything but peace. As a Christian, I felt it necessary to represent Christ in a positive light and to 'think' before I acted, even though I may have been justified in behaving in the negative way I often witness on that small stretch of road. I was mindful that my children were watching me and would potentially mirror my reaction to unexpected drama. Although it felt positive not to have succumbed to the urge to boisterously reprimand her publicly on the street corner, I still felt a sense of panic and worry inside, as I now had another problem on my hands that I didn't create or need. As I drove to the dealership, anxiety really began to set in, as I had only a short window to obtain the quote and be back in time for my son's optician appointment. I felt this sense of anxiety begin to heighten as time was now dwindling, and I also couldn't get through to my husband on the phone. By this time, my blood was beginning to boil, and that state of calm I had displayed to everyone else around me it seems was not enough to last.

With minutes to spare, I received the £500 quote from the dealership and rushed to the optician appointment, calling them on the way to let them know I would be late. During the appointment, I found myself unable to concentrate, as I was busy relaying the events to my husband, who had finally answered the phone. When I got home that evening, I called Lisa to explain my findings. She said she would speak to her partner who worked nights, and would text me that night once she had been in contact with him, irrespective of the time, to check whether or not it is too late to call me with an update. She again apologised profusely and thanked me for being so understanding. She promised that she would call me the next morning in order to get the ball rolling.

I went to bed quite peaceful that night, content that I could display the type of mercy I would like to receive had I been the perpetrator of such an event. I woke up in the middle of the night quite suddenly, checked my phone, and was disappointed not to see a text from Lisa, as promised. I found myself beginning to feel worried that this was a sign that she was not in fact a woman of her word, and that perhaps she would try to "scam me" in the way she said that she would not. Even so, I quickly dispelled those negative thoughts and forced myself back to sleep, trying not to jump to conclusions, hopeful that she would indeed call me in the morning, as previously stated. I woke up at 4:23am to continue working on this book, aware that it was unlikely she would be up this early, and expected to potentially hear from her from 8:00am onwards. At this point, I felt fairly peaceful and pretty much continued on with the tasks for the day. 9:00am went by, so did 10:00am, 11:00am and 12:00pm, and I hadn't yet received a phone call. I spoke to my husband and we both tried to give her the benefit of the doubt, but when it became afternoon, I felt it necessary to call her to get an update on the situation. By this time, my mind began wondering whether my kindness had been taken for weakness, and my blood again began to simmer.

When I called her at 12:27pm that afternoon, she declined to answer my phone call by pressing 'No' on her phone; she also did the same when we called from my husband's phone at 4:37pm that same afternoon. I sent her a text to politely ask her to contact me immediately but I did not receive a reply. After this time, it began to look as though Lisa had crashed into my car, said she would take responsibility for it, yet was now purposefully avoiding me. Peace had left me and the temperature of my simmering blood suddenly began to skyrocket. I felt completely taken advantage of and upset began to fester. The saying "When a person shows you who they are the first time, believe them" began to feel as though it was ringing true. My mind then went into overdrive with negative thoughts about what course of action to take next. I became preoccupied with listening out for a ringing phone and found it increasingly hard to enjoy the small moments with my family on the first day of the Christmas holiday.

Come evening time, I called my sister and mother to vent. The issue for me wasn't the damage to the car; it was the fact that I had behaved in good faith towards this lady and she had now appeared to be taking liberties. A simple update from her would have alleviated all of my fears. As I began to regret being merciful towards her, my family reminded me not to *"grow weary of doing good"* (Galatians 6:9, ESV), as the Bible outlines. However, at this point, since Lisa had proven herself untrustworthy, we felt it imperative to take formal action against her to safeguard myself from being liable for the damage.

Regaining Lost Peace

On reflection, I had realised a few important points that helped me in regaining the peace I had lost.

On thinking a little more deeply about the situation, it became apparent that I had allowed the fact that Lisa had failed to text or call as promised and her avoidance of my calls later on to encourage me jump to a number of negative and unfounded conclusions. I automatically assumed that since she had fallen short of her promises and was so in awe of how patient I had been, she was now being intentionally disrespectful towards me and would not pay for the damages as she had stated. On reflection however, I believe that it was premature to draw such a definitive conclusion and to, in turn, allow my thoughts to run away with me, further increasing the frustration I had felt. There was a brief moment where I had considered that the nearing of Christmas meant it would be unlikely that Lisa had such a high amount of disposable income available. Perhaps she was simply trying to figure out where she would obtain the finances from and needed extra time. Yes, she could have updated me if this was the case, but perhaps there was a reason why she couldn't that I was not yet privy to and she would hopefully be in touch in due course.

I also recognised that my perspective of the situation was key in determining whether or not I could experience peace. I realised that the situation itself did not feel as frustrating as the aftermath, and after a pep talk from my husband, it was clear that I had allowed a 'not so serious situation' the power to rob me of all of my peace. In this moment, I recalled a quote from a reality TV millionaire who was about to be sued by a disgruntled former employee. When asked if she was worried about the impending case, she said, "No, I don't need to. I pay lawyers to handle these things for me." Although I may not be a millionaire yet, I have paid insurance brokers thousands of pounds over the last 18 years, and in the same vein, "They can handle this for me." Once my perspective shifted, I felt more at peace.

That evening, as I sat on the bedroom floor, wrapping the remaining Christmas presents for our loved ones, I felt compelled to pray to God for peace. I then played some gospel music in the background, which helped lessen my feelings of frustration. When I began to focus more on God's goodness than the nature of this problem, this created room for peace to begin to enter in.

During the latter part of this same evening, I received a phone call from a cancer survivor friend who told me that his cancer may have returned. Suddenly, my problem no longer felt to be as bad, and I opened my heart to peace again.

I used my experience above to outline as transparently as possible that as human beings, when unexpected drama arises in our lives, there may always be things that we could have done better. The thing is, when a situation is completely out of your control, you will never experience true peace unless there is true surrender. By true surrender, I mean getting to the stage where you fully, not partially, surrender the outcome to God with no conditions or caveats around it. How you behave in the midst of the unknowing paints an accurate picture of just how much peace it is that you truly have inside of you. As I approach a new year, I am in the process of exploring how to better deal with unexpected drama, and to be less affected by it when it does arise. When put into perspective, things could really have been a lot worse. I asked myself, "How did I behave when faced with unexpected drama? What could I do differently to help me better hold onto peace?" Perhaps you can ask yourself the same questions.

Learning from Experience

What type of situations generally rob you of your peace?

_____

_____

_____

_____

What practical things could you do to reduce frustration and gain peace quicker?

_____

_____

_____

_____

Sometimes, it is possible to avoid certain situations. Is it possible to avoid these situations or lessen the likelihood that you collide with them? If so, how?

_____
_____
_____
_____

List one situation where you have been faced with unexpected drama and not felt at peace:

_____
_____
_____
_____

What is your general pattern of thinking and subsequent response when faced with such a crisis?

_____
_____
_____
_____

If you could relive that situation again, what would you do differently?

_____
_____
_____
_____

Ideally, what would it look like to feel at peace when in crisis?

_____
_____
_____
_____

What examples of peace in crisis from those closest to you have you witnessed?

_____
_____
_____
_____

List one situation where you have been in crisis and you have managed to cultivate some peace:

_____
_____
_____
_____

How did you cultivate this peace and maintain it?

What learning could you apply to future similar situations?

What area(s) do you most need to experience peace in now?

What would be the benefits of possessing peace in your life now?

What may you have to surrender in order to gain peace?

_____

_____

_____

_____

Even though I was reluctant to write about this scenario at the time it occurred, I experienced it to be therapeutic in nature. Furthermore, putting pen to paper helped me to recognise how I could learn and grow from this experience and what tools I could use if faced with a similar situation. This prompted a shift in perspective and a decision to be 'ok' with whatever the outcome was. Sure enough, once I had 'let it go', I received a text from Lisa the following morning, apologising for the delay in response and explaining that she didn't have the finances this side of Christmas. She supplied me with her insurance policy number to begin processing the claim. Ironically, the insurance company offered me £250 extra to compensate me for my trouble. It seems that God does indeed have a way of turning the negative things that happen to us into positives, when we fully surrender the outcome to Him and His purpose (Romans 8:28, NIV).

As humans, we often allow unexpected drama, other individuals, our past, our present circumstances or anxiety about the future to rob us of our peace. I can appreciate that this example is not as severe as some of the other scenarios that you may be facing at present. Regardless of how powerful your urge to give up is, the sentiments stay the same; try your best to put things into perspective and do everything you can to hold onto peace. If your peace is predicated by the actions of others towards you or external uncontrollable events, you will forever be at the mercy of things you cannot control. Whilst watching the Rio 2016 Olympics with my husband, two American swimmers who won the silver medal had a stance that illustrated this perfectly. They told the world on live TV that because their identity was in Jesus Christ, win or lose, they had peace. Affirmation for them was not rooted in whether or not the world hailed them as Olympians. Affirmation for them was knowing and believing that Jesus Christ loved them regardless. Because of this peace, they were able to choose joy, and as a result, they were unshakeable, regardless of the result. The same can be true for you when you stumble upon unexpected drama. Even if like me, you have to engage in an initial internal battle to maintain peace, it is a fight worth winning. I have learnt that peace is in fact a choice; you either want it, or you don't. If you believe that peace is truly attainable and give your all to see it manifest, you are already halfway to receiving it.

Peace Within

Thus far, we have considered the pursuit of peace and how our thoughts, feelings, daily routines and unexpected drama can negatively or positively impact the intensity of peace experienced in various areas of our life. We are now about to delve into the main crux of this book; the five key areas in which we most desire a sense of peace. The first, 'peace within', is probably the most important, as without an inner sense of peace, it is unlikely that it will translate to any other area of your life. Inner peace is that type of 'any weather' rather than only a 'fair weather' sense of tranquility. Contrary to popular belief, no matter what we have been through in life, 'any weather peace' is available to us all.

For example, in my clinical work, I have heard clients from all different walks of life doubt they will ever experience inner peace in their adult life, simply because of the absence of peace during their childhood. Common statements against the possibility of present day peace include: "I don't expect to feel peace at all, you know, because I grew up in care" or "When he touched me as a child, he took away any chance of me ever experiencing peace on the inside", or lastly, "Abandoned children never grow into peaceful adults." Although many clients toy with the idea of actively searching for inner peace, a large majority don't because of the long held belief that they are doomed to failure before they even begin. They believe that not being fortunate enough to experience a 'peaceful beginning' in life disqualifies them from ever being able to fraternise with peace in the future. While the beginning of your life may have been out of your control, the present and the future are not, and peace on the inside can be yours, if you first believe and then take action to claim it. This chapter will uncover and dispel the myth that peace within is only available to those with a perfect start in life. If this were true, many of us, myself included, would only be able to dream of ever experiencing it.

As a psychotherapist, there is a common misconception that we always have and always will 'have it all together'. For me, this could not be further from the truth. I stumbled upon a quote recently from one of the richest men alive, Bill Gates, which reads: *"If you are born poor, it's not your mistake, but if you die poor, it's your mistake."* I believe that the same can be said for the state of peace you accumulate throughout your lifetime. I have come to learn that not having a peaceful beginning in life does not have to mean that peace remains a foreign concept in your days ahead. Perhaps unearthing a little about my early-lived experience, especially pertaining to difficulties with my upbringing and my race, will help shed some light on the matter.

A Not so Peaceful Beginning

I was born in London on a crisp March morning in the 1980s. My mother is a St Lucian born British migrant, and my father, a British born man of Jamaican heritage. As the youngest of three children, although I don't remember everything about our early years as a family of five, I am certain that a series of unpleasant events caused my mother to grab her three small children and singlehandedly flee from my father in the middle of the night, with nothing but the clothes on our backs. In our new life that lay ahead, for my Black childhood peers and I, being Black as a child in the 1980s meant a life tinged with the stench of socio-economic deprivation, abusive and absent fathers, and struggling single parent households.

As I recount, I attempt to ignore the feeling of heaviness present in the middle of my chest. It feels to be prompting my throat to burn, the sensation that often precedes falling tears that one wishes to stem. I find myself conflicted with telling an authentic story, having the ugly truth laid bare, and protecting my mother in a way my father did not. Peace is feeling a little hard to hold onto at the moment. Still, for you to truly comprehend how a non-peaceful beginning in life does not disqualify you from experiencing peace now, unearthing the truth about my early-lived experience is non-negotiable.

My personal experience of being Black in early childhood then meant witnessing frequent injustice in the ill treatment of the undervalued Black woman at the hands of the Black man, whilst feeling powerless to stop it. The impact of this on my subsequent sense of being Black led to uncertainty about whether Blacks could be trusted to support other Blacks, encouraging questions about my worth and value. As you can imagine, although I may not have been conscious of it at the time, internal peace seemed to elude me, as it did my client, William, aforementioned in the introduction.

In growing up in a predominantly Black community in London, 'difference' was not something I often encountered. At times, I wondered what it would be like forming friendships with other races, because I had often found my Black primary school peers to be unpredictable in their loyalty towards me, willing to 'turn on me' in order to remain as part of the in-crowd. The notion of injustice and powerlessness in my home, it seems, had also found its way into the 'sameness' in the school playground. This feeling of 'sameness', however, would disappear somewhat when my mother would take us on excursions outside of the borough for nature walks in Hampstead Heath. It was as though sentiments of the undervaluing of Blacks involved in the atrocities of slavery had in some way manifested itself in the 'posh' parts of West London. I experienced during these times what it felt like to be in a minority, based only upon the colour of my skin. Long and cautious stares from children with blue or green eyes towards my dark brown eyes and skin was something I had never felt comfortable with. The physical drawing away of White middle class children and their parents always left me feeling as though we had ventured into territory in which we did not belong. The effect of this on me as a child was questioning whether the difference between us meant that something was undesirable about *me*. This difference was never experienced positively. It felt as though being White was the 'gold standard', and that anything else was perceived to be subpar. As you can imagine, a sense of inner peace and complete self-acceptance was not something I was able to foster during this time.

In an attempt to alter the potential mediocre trajectory of my life, my mother enrolled me in a secondary school in the leafy suburbs of Hertfordshire, inhabited by a predominantly White community with a subculture of their own. By this time, she had worked tirelessly to undo the negative picture painted of what it meant to be a Black single mother, making great strides in her academic pursuits and subsequently accumulating great wealth. Despite her good intentions, the next five years for me involved having to endure monkey chants on the train, having my afro bunches and big lips ridiculed, being referred to as a "Black bitch" or a "Nigga", and being spat at by other White children as though we were rubbish, like African slaves casually thrown overboard from the edge of the transatlantic slave ships. Peace at this stage was anywhere but within me.

Although presented in a more covert fashion, racial prejudice was also rife within the White teaching staff I had longed to find solace in. Assertion in Black children was always misinterpreted as insolence by White staff, in the same way the term 'angry Black woman' has been freely portrayed by the media. "*You people* are so difficult," my balding, elderly Caucasian science teacher shouted, as he pointed at my group of Black peers and I. Pre-judgments and labelling followed. "Oh, *you're Selone*," teachers would comment upon first meeting me. It felt as though these pre-judgments had robbed me of any opportunity to demonstrate positive attributes, dooming me to failure prematurely. As a Black teenager, I felt very isolated and unsupported by staff and students alike, which made it more challenging to apply myself in education. The prejudice experienced also negatively impacted interpersonal interaction and gave rise to feelings of invisibility and worthlessness, just like research on Black men attempting to grapple with societal injustice in the US (Franklin, 1999; Franklin, 2004; Franklin & Boyd-Franklin, 2000; Word, Zanna & Cooper 1974). Being Black during secondary school then meant being in the minority, perceived to be incapable of academic success, being ostracised and marginalised, feared aggressive, negatively labelled, misinterpreted and misunderstood, discriminated against, and easier to control if Black gatherings were prohibited. On the outside, I put on a brave face, but on the inside, peace was absent.

By this stage, it became apparent that a lot of the struggles I experienced unfortunately correlated heavily with the brown shade of skin I had been born into. Having to endure such ill treatment at school, based only on the colour of my skin, was more difficult than words could describe. Sadly, similar themes also featured in a more subtle manner in various areas of my adult life. To have to toy with such disturbing thoughts about worth, belonging and powerlessness whilst directly experiencing discrimination and deprivation as a child was a difficult environment for peace to exist in, let alone thrive. Despite the absence of a father, the presence of a loving, God-fearing and affirming mother went a long way in helping to protect me from all the debris of difficulty that would blow towards me as soon as I would step foot outside the front door. I began to realise however that as the world grew colder and home felt further and further away, *I* would have to take responsibility for developing *my own* sense of peace, taking it with me inside my heart to any good or bad new place I would venture.

We All Have a Choice

In regards to my story, I can acknowledge that although much of my experience of being Black in relation to others has been negative, there have also been many positives. Whether these previous negative experiences allow me to overthink about what the 'other' *may* or *may not* think about me, or prompt me to behave in an unkind manner towards others of a different or similar race is a choice *I* had to make (Lichtenstein, 2003). I decided that the racial prejudice of a few or the abuse my mother suffered at the hands of *my* father would not mar what could be to come with other non-Black individuals I encountered or any Black men sincerely looking for love. Perhaps in time you will also be able to bring any similar negative thoughts to consciousness, dispel them, and judge new scenarios independently, leading with openness and optimism. In this pursuit of peace, I have found love. Despite all I have experienced at the hands of the 'other', I still love those who I should hate, and I credit my Christianity for this.

When difficult circumstances happen to us in our early or adult lives, there is a natural tendency for anger, sadness or hopelessness to consciously or unconsciously bubble under the surface within us. Although these thoughts and feelings may seem justified, they do nothing to help you in your pursuit of inner peace. Instead, harbouring feelings of resentment and unforgiveness towards the perpetrator of a horrendous event is like *you* drinking poison and hoping that the *other person* dies. Rather than experiencing peace, it is likely you will find yourself in a million pieces, scattered and separated in that broken place, unsure of how to glue yourself back together.

Peace is Still Available

In my role as a psychotherapist, I have walked through many a dark day where clients sit with me and recount in great detail repressed or very present painful memories of sexual abuse as children. Because God's plans for you are *"for good and not disaster"* (Jeremiah 29:11, NLT), *"your adversary, the devil, walks about like a roaring lion, seeking whom he may devour"* (1 Peter 5:8, NKJV). Childhood sexual abuse is simply one method the devil uses, which can be powerful enough to knock generations off the course God had planned for them. The abuse can be so impactful that it need only occur once and the return on investment can last a lifetime, destroying any belief that anything good can come from something so bad. This is a lie; shame and guilt of a crime you did not commit need not hold you hostage for the rest of your life. Just like in Zechariah 3 (NIV), Christ covers our shameful feelings, similar to Him clothing the High Priest in clean robes, even whilst the devil accused him before God's throne. The sad thing is, not everyone is privy to this, or they find it difficult to believe it, even when they are aware. Subsequently, within circumstances of childhood sexual abuse, the adult victims of such trauma I have worked with tend to fall into three specific categories, as outlined below. Unfortunately, the majority I have encountered remain in category one, where there is no hope of peace for the future.

Category One

Some individuals are still tormented with this early suffering, who appear to be 'stuck' at the age that this horrific incident occurred. Due to the difficulty in accepting that in many cases, 'a loved one' could have sought to remove their childlike innocence, denial that the events actually occurred often features. Many of these memories have been repressed to the degree that access to them is at best, hazy, and at worst, near impossible. This often precedes a sense of powerlessness to dream about brighter days ahead, accompanied by a feeling that this individual is still mentally and emotionally under the control and subjection of their now absent abuser.

Category Two

In contrast, other sufferers of sexual abuse are able to accept the occurrence of these difficult events and begin to process the impact at a slow but comfortable pace for them. These individuals may undertake much of this work inwardly and privately, going back and forth through different thoughts and emotions for a lengthy period of time. They desire peace and begin an uncertain and tumultuous journey in pursuit of it.

Category Three

Lastly, there are a group of clients I have worked with who have acknowledged that although these unfortunate events did happen to them, they do not have the power to define who they are now. Some of these individuals have even gone so far as to 'make their pain pay' by setting up empowerment services for victims of sexual abuse, writing books, and running international seminars on how to recover and excel in the face of childhood sexual trauma. Despite what happened to them, they have refused to allow their chance of peace within to be swept from under their feet, as they have already paid a high price for the sins of others, and don't believe they should continue to suffer.

As a psychotherapist, I have learnt not to favour one group over the other, or to rush them along in their processing of the difficulties they have experienced in early life. In willing them to foster and sustain lasting peace within themselves, my job is simply to highlight that *they do* have the power to choose peace at the time they feel is most appropriate for them, and like Rogers (1957), my person-centred base reminds me of the belief that the clients themselves already have the answer.

Introducing: The Prince of Peace

All of the above sounds great, but I must be clear in highlighting that this does require work. It required work for me to reject the negative labels and unfavourable treatment based on the colour of my skin. Despite witnessing the abuse of the Black woman at the hands of the Black man, akin to Africans enslaving other Africans, I also had to reject the belief that this needs to be part and parcel of who I am and will become. I chose to acknowledge it, let it go and choose peace. Let it go? Choose peace? That makes it sound so easy, right? When I refer to letting it go, this for me meant no longer being willing to carry the excess weight that had been bound to my neck for many years, pulling me down as I sought to elevate up the steep mountain climb. Perhaps, like you, I began to experience extreme fatigue, carrying a heavy load, sweating profusely, and longing for a sip of water to help alleviate my struggles as I trudged alone through the sand dunes of the Sahara desert. I often dreamed of a time when these weights would just miraculously float off into the atmosphere and I would not have to face the fact that, like cancer, these difficulties were starting to spread, increasing the likelihood that other areas of my life would soon become affected. In hindsight, it is evident that this thinking was unrealistic, as the laws of gravity and the heaviness of the load involved would not allow this idea to manifest. The only viable remedy for a tangible pursuit of inner peace first required becoming acquainted with the *"prince of peace"*, Jesus Christ (Isaiah 9:6, NKJV). Beginning a real journey of peace involved a letting go and a stripping off of every weight that had been slowing me down (Hebrews 12:1, NLT). What did I do with these weights and burdens? I laid them all at the feet of Christ.

A quote from Matthew 11:28-30 (TPT) reads:

"Are you weary, carrying a heavy burden? Then come to me. I will refresh your life, for I am your oasis. Simply join your life with mine. Learn my ways and you'll discover that I'm gentle, humble, easy to please. You will find refreshment and rest in me. For all that I require of you will be pleasant and easy to bear."

At first glance, this sounds like an opportunity not to be missed. Jesus Christ is inviting us to come to Him when things are feeling tough. However, if finding peace were as easy as this scripture conveys, everyone who is aware of it would have accepted it. Considering the state of dismay even some Christians find themselves in, there must be more to this story. You see, the society and culture we live in credits those who appear to have everything under control. To have to relinquish control and give it over to a God that you cannot see or physically touch is a concept many people have trouble comprehending. Although you cannot see God, I have come to find that like a toothache, I can feel God and I know that He is there. Still, it would be naive of me not to acknowledge that accepting this invitation for peace would at first require an admission that all is not well in paradise. Pride and the pursuit of peace cannot co-exist. A laying down of one's burdens and difficulties at the feet of Christ for a proud person is therefore no easy feat. If the perception you hold of yourself (or which others hold of you) is that, like me, you are assumed to 'have it all together', this will be an exceptionally difficult task for you. The very essence of handing over our issues to God requires an exposure of our vulnerabilities and a level of submission that society has taught us not to be comfortable with. One thing to note however, is that Jesus never asks us to do something He has never done Himself. In sacrificing Himself on the cross so that we might be free from sin and live an eternal and abundant life, He Himself hung on this cross exposed, vulnerable, and submitted to the will of God.

Over time, I weighed up the cost of being vulnerable, and I submitted to Christ against the constant agony of trying to manage my relentless pain by myself. I felt it futile to continue to reject an offer of complete freedom. As I stood metaphorically on the platform, unable to board the train to destiny due to the weight and cluster of my unnecessary bags, something dawned on me. I recognised it would benefit *me* to hand these bags over to someone else with body-builder type muscles, who cares for me more deeply than anyone else on planet Earth. This allowed me to sit more comfortably on the train, rejuvenated and clear-headed, alert enough not to miss my stop. The next phase of life for me then would involve running freely through the meadow in the spring sunshine, with the wind blowing effortlessly through my flowing tresses, unscathed by the multitude of bugs that had lodged themselves in my cardigan, no longer side tracked by insignificant things seeking to derail me from pursuing all of the great things He had called me to be.

Put simply, once I handed over my issues to Jesus Christ, I found peace within. What was once my problem now became His problem, and He was happy and able to manage it for me. I have now become more aware of situations that are likely to rob me of my peace and I avoid them. If they cannot be avoided, I have become more conscious of the feeling that my peace is starting to falter and, in practical terms, my first response is always to speak to God. It simply involves uttering a little prayer whenever I feel the need. It doesn't need to be fancy or eloquent, God is simply delighted to hear from me, and you. My communication with God normally sounds a little something like:

"God, thank you for being good to me, despite my imperfections. Thank you for being available for me to talk to you at any time of the day or night. I'm sorry for anything I have done to hurt you. This thing that I'm going through right now is trying to rob me of my peace. Just as you said in your Word, I am leaving this burden with you and you will give me rest."

Even though I didn't have an initial peaceful beginning in life, it was possible to gain some perspective on the beginning I did experience, and to create a more peaceful present and future. The same can be true for you.

Maybe laying your burdens at the feet of Christ is a good place for you to start.

Images of Peace

Get a piece of paper and draw an image that represents what difficult periods in your life have signified for you. It may be scribbles, objects, or an actual scene.

What feeling does looking at your current picture conjure up?

_____
_____
_____
_____

On another piece of paper, regardless of what is going on in your life now, draw a depiction of what you desire your days ahead to look like in terms of inner peace.

When you hold these pictures side by side, what differences or similarities do you notice?

_____

_____

_____

_____

The bible reminds us to *"speak of things that don't yet exist as if they are real"* (Romans 4:17, ERV). In other words, believing that peace is possible makes the receiving of peace a plausible reality. Even if it feels hard to imagine a life as tranquil as your second picture (if you felt able to draw one at this stage), the fact that you are reading this book is a start in the right direction to finding peace within yourself. Keep this second picture in a safe place, or place it up on a notice board, glancing at it every so often as a reminder of what you are heading towards. A non-peaceful beginning or experiencing non-peaceful situations throughout your life does not have to cheat you out of experiencing peace now. Even when there is no reason to hope, I urge you to keep on hoping; peace inside of you is on the way (Romans 4:18, NLT).

Health Wise

In looking at 'peace within' in the previous chapter, we have learnt that difficult or traumatic circumstances are enough for some people to be knocked off course and to close the lid on the thought of finding peace on the inside. The same can be true of our health. Sometimes nature deals us an unfortunate card by way of illness or disease, and everything in life can feel to be brought to an immediate and unexpected halt. Finding and maintaining peace in your health for the most part is something that *is* within our control. Sometimes, however, when nature does decide to dish out some of its nastiest and most destructive disorders, although it may feel hard to hold onto, peace can still be yours. After all, I recently watched an advert, which portrayed different individuals suffering with cancer. Instead of having them laid up in a hospital bed, heavily drugged and tied up to various machines, waiting for death to overtake them, it depicted a mother playing with her children in the park and a husband and wife in bed together after they had shared an intimate moment. The slogan read: 'A mother with cancer is still a mother' and 'A lover with cancer is still a lover'. In essence, this meant that despite the illness they were facing, they were still who they were before, and life must continue to go on in the best and most peaceful way possible. If ever you are faced with some difficulties with your health, hopefully this chapter will help to give you the right perspective on how to move forward. Either way, it will remind you just how precious your health is, encourage you to make wiser health related choices and will give you ideas on how to better invest in it.

Seemingly 'Fit and Healthy'

Robert was a fit and healthy 31-year-old family friend who was unexpectedly diagnosed with Primary Sclerosing Cholangitis (PSC), a rare, incurable, chronic liver disease. Liver damage is often associated with alcohol abuse, but specialists maintain PSC is in no way related to alcohol, especially since, in this case, Robert had always been teetotal. As the disease quickly and fiercely progressed, Robert suffered from drastic weight loss, debilitating itching, extreme fatigue, and excruciating abdominal pain. His once fast-paced life as a successful football agent was now playing in slow motion as he watched a well-known wealthy celebrity being robbed of life at the hands of this same disease. PSC does not discriminate based on age, race or gender, and worse than all of these physical symptoms was the mental and emotional unrest in feeling and looking as though death was knocking at his door.

As Robert's condition began to deteriorate, he was put on the liver transplant list. Having someone die who had been thoughtful enough to ensure that someone else could live on was his only form of hope. This was made worse by the fact that his blood group was extremely rare, making his chances of finding a suitable match at this advanced stage of his disease near to impossible. We had many conversations during this time about the fragility of life, and acknowledged that although he had been blessed with an abundance of finances, this simply wasn't a problem that money could solve. His health was his wealth, and since that was deteriorating, real capital was of no use. The only currency he had to trade in was his faith. Robert's faith in Jesus Christ gave him peace. We spoke earlier about having an unmovable anchor in times of distress; for Robert, this was his faith in Christ. Did we have many a tearful conversation together and skim briefly over the "What ifs"? Sure we did. But the peace found in focusing on the promises littered throughout God's Word was what held him through that year of waiting to be given another chance at life on the liver transplant list. Sure enough, a year to the exact same date that he was added to the donor list, at 3:44am, awoken from sleep, he received a phone call from the hospital from a health advisor named Rebecca. She explained in a direct and calm manner that a suitable liver had been found for him and that he should make his way to the hospital immediately.

Did Robert have some worries during his testing ordeal? Of course, but he didn't allow them to take over and further disrupt any sense of joy he had left in life. As you will see below, worry and illness or the mere thought of illness do not go well together.

Self-Diagnosis

As a twenty-something-year-old fit and healthy young lady, in June a number of years ago, my family and I had just saved up enough money to have a holiday abroad whilst being on maternity leave. It was a much-needed family break after adjusting to the life of a full-time milk cow (breastfeeding mother) again, but this time with two young children under my care. Though the sun was hot, the breeze was cool and the environment was as peace inducing as you can ever imagine, my mind felt as turbulent as the recent plane ride we had undertaken. It was as though my handbag containing my passport had been stolen, whilst being stuck in a foreign, cold country on a rainy and thundery day without an umbrella or a clue of how I would be getting home. I wasn't sick, but after feeling a few tingles in my body, I had convinced myself I was. My negative and anti-social mood and constant day dreaming about how this illness would now affect our future was beginning to ruin our present. My husband was as usual very supportive in helping to rationalise my fears, but honestly speaking, he was fighting a losing battle, as I had allowed worry to taint the lenses of my sunglasses even further. It was like being in sunshine but allowing a thick cloud of smog to obscure my vision, spoiling the experience for everyone else that I claimed to love.

After finding out that the hotel Wi-Fi was not in fact free, as per their holiday advert, I still spent endless hours and money on Google researching my symptoms, wasting money that could have been used to buy necessities like nappies or wipes. In that moment, I had become 'Dr. Ajewole', self-diagnosing, searching for the worst-case scenario and internalising the idea that my fate was doomed. Even though I was in paradise, in actuality, I had allowed my mind to live in a third world, poverty-stricken and diseased-ridden land with no hope of change. After undergoing some tests back in England, it turned out that the tingles I had been experiencing were simply harmless side effects from the C-section I had undergone a few months prior and in fact I was well. On reflection, my attempt to self-diagnose gave rise to worry, and this unfounded worry was strong enough to ruin our holiday. As you will see below, this type of self-diagnosis is also wreaking havoc on our health system, and, if left to continue, may have dire consequences for humanity as we know it.

"I Think I'm Sick, Give Me Drugs!"

This rising culture of internet self-diagnosis is inadvertently encouraging us as a nation to drain the resources of the National Health Service (NHS), whereby we turn up at the doctor's surgery at the first sign of a sore throat, demanding to be screened for oesophageal cancer. I watched a programme a few years ago on BBC1, entitled *The Doctor Who Gave Up Drugs*. As an Infection Doctor, he was well versed on the type of infections that the human body can be plagued with and the limits that traditional medicine has on healing them. He was concerned that current day society tends to opt for drugs as a first response for issues as simple as the common cold. He conducted research to highlight that in the majority of cases, if the doctor is not completely sure the infection is bacterial rather than viral, prescribing antibiotics could actually do a patient more harm than good. He undertook an experiment to prove to a lady, who had been plagued with shoulder and back pain for 20 years, that the dangerous cocktail of prescription painkillers she had been on for the same amount of time was actually having no effect. Similarly, a depressed mother of one, who had been on anti-depressants from the ages of 16 to 24 and still felt depressed, wanted to figure out if there were other ways to alleviate her symptoms.

The doctor opened their mind to the healing power of regular physical exercise, with astounding results. As a psychotherapist, I would have highlighted the healing power of talking therapies in addition to physical exercise to help further induce a state of peace and tranquility whilst on their uphill journey. Moreover, I believe that regular quiet moments can also be an overlooked preventative method or even a cure for a foggy mind. A stroll in nature, a warm bath, relaxing music or an afternoon nap can all go a long way to minimise tension and bring about peace.

By using a special machine that tested the blood of patients requesting antibiotics, the doctor was able to prove that the infection was simply viral, and wrote a prescription for honey and lemon, physically handing this to each patient with a James Bond DVD, to rest with whilst they recovered. I'm not sure how well this change would be accepted in practice if it was rolled out within the wider NHS, but from growing up in a home in which our mother would administer herbal rather than traditional medicine, with great results and no unwanted side effects, I would definitely advocate this way of dealing with physical illness as a first response when the appropriate research has been conducted and it is in the best interest of the patient.

Taking Things for Granted?

So as we can see, good health is precious. Unfortunately, however, it is something that a lot of us take for granted until it is threatened or taken away. Having peace in your health is not something any of us can guarantee, as, like Robert, we are all susceptible to being struck with an unexpected, life-threatening illness. That being said, however, we can all do small things every day to ensure that our own actions have not caused or increased the likelihood that we are faced with health issues that were in fact avoidable.

Good physical health is the basis by which you function well in every other area in your life. Without a healthy body, it is extremely challenging and, in some cases, nearly impossible to undertake the most simple of tasks. I was guilty of taking my fully functioning limbs for granted until I could no longer butter a piece of toast, write notes during a university lecture or wash my own hair, after my right arm became injured in a minor car crash. The same can be said of the mind. The majority of clients I work with on a daily basis spend the 50 minutes allocated appointment time trying to figure out how to alleviate sickness or unrest in the mind. In a number of my clients who present with issues of anxiety or depression, as described in earlier chapters, these issues begin in their mind, take root, and then filter out into their behaviours. By employing Cognitive Behavioural techniques (CBT), for example, clients become more aware of their cognitions or thoughts, which subsequently affects their behaviours, in an attempt to bring about appropriately paced change.

Getting Physical

In trying not to take good health for granted, when speaking about physical exercise, which best describes you? Couch potato or fitness fanatic? Or perhaps you may fall somewhere in between? I know, I know, you've heard it all before, exercise helps you feel better, look better and live longer. So why is it so difficult for many to commit to the recommended 150 minutes over 5 days?

Like many people, I once felt I didn't have enough time to exercise, and the result was a more fuller and sluggish version of my once extremely petite frame. I'm at a place now where I cannot afford NOT to exercise. With improving my sleeping habits and being creative with my workouts, I was able to find a system that worked for me. A few tips include:

- **Get inspired:** Watching YouTube videos or speaking to real life people who have made a healthy transition through diet and exercise often gives us the motivation required to see what is possible. Use these individuals' stories as healthy inspiration only, rather than the benchmark, as your journey will be unique to yourself.
- **Wake up earlier to exercise:** Instead of draining you, exercising first thing in the morning on an empty stomach gives you the kick and energy you need to start the day. Besides, many undisciplined

people who say they will exercise in the evening don't. If you do it in the morning, you don't have to think about it for the rest of the day. If however waking up earlier is so taxing that it is counterproductive, perhaps you could consider choosing a gym or sports centre near work and commit to exercising before you go home and relax for the evening.

- **Do shorter workouts more frequently:** Workouts don't have to be long. This can include a 30-minute brisk walk or jog, a 25-minute workout DVD, 20 minutes of swimming, a 30-minute YouTube workout video, etc. Consider engaging in these a few times a week.

- **Be consistent:** There is a slogan by a workout DVD company called Beach Body, which states: 'Decide, Commit, Succeed.' Once individuals have internalised this ideology, oftentimes, there is no stopping them, and they complete a full 60-day workout programme such as Insanity by Shaun T. The problem is, once the duration of the programme is over, they rightly celebrate their achievement but fail to continue with a consistent workout regimen. What happens after this? Unfortunately, they find themselves back where they started. Don't forget, consistency is key!

- **Find an accountability partner:** Some people commit better to exercising frequently when they have someone they are either working out with or who they are accountable to. Find whichever works for you and reap the rewards.

- **Take before and after pictures:** Taking down body measurements such as your weight and the inches around your body can be used as a good way to track progress. However, for some people, regularly measuring progress using this method can feel counterproductive and discouraging if, for instance, it appears that you haven't lost weight when you may have gained the fat you lost right back in muscle. Using photos and being cognizant of the changes in how your clothes fit as a measure of your progress can provide more motivation for many individuals. Remember to celebrate even small achievements.

Eating Clean

In addition to physical exercise, it is also important to draw attention to either the healing or destructive power of the type of food we put into our bodies. The type of food we consume is akin to putting the right type of fuel in a car. If we put the wrong type of fuel in a car, it is likely to break down. We need to be intentional about watching what and how we eat so that we can maximise the quality of life for both ourselves and those we love around us.

What is Eating Clean?

Rather than a diet, Eating Clean is a sustainable lifestyle change that gives you and your family the energy needed to live a vibrant and energetic life. It doesn't require you to omit certain food groups or starve yourself in between meals. Rather, it involves eating more, yet weighing less simply by choosing the right types of food to eat.

At its core, Eating Clean entails eating a balanced diet in small portions of clean (unprocessed) foods every few hours for optimal health. This consists of eating 5-6 small meals per day, pairing complex carbohydrates with lean protein. Replacing all white breads, pastas, rice, etc. with wholemeal versions ensures your body is receiving the type of carbohydrates that sustain energy, rather than deplete you of it. This type of eating also ignites your metabolism, allowing you to burn fat more easily. Do you have to eat perfectly 100% of the time? No! It is important to allow yourself to indulge in a treat once in a while, giving you something to look forward to. With these small changes, clients, friends and family, as well as myself, have all reported feeling as though they have a new lease on life.

If Eating Clean does not sound like it's for you, there are many resources on the internet and in the library with more information on eating a balanced diet; all you have to do is search for it and put it into action. One good way to start may be by giving up one thing you love that you know does not help you in trying to attain peace in your health, replacing it with a healthier alternative. For example, you may want to give up fizzy drink and try replacing this with unprocessed fruit juice, and then, in time, water. Below are a few Eat Clean Meal Plan examples for you to get started with.

Eat Clean One Day Meal Plan Example:

Breakfast

Food: Oats with Blueberries and Almond Milk

Drink: Lemon Water

Snack

Food: Apple Slices with Organic Peanut Butter

Drink: Water

Lunch

Food: Egg, Avocado and Mozzarella Salad inside Wholemeal Tortilla Wrap

Drink: Pure Apple Juice

Snack

Food: Handful of Cashew Nuts

Drink: Spinach, Carrot, Strawberry, Banana, Ginger Smoothie with Vanilla Rice Milk

Dinner

Food: Baked Salmon Fillet, Vegetables, Brown Rice

Drink: Water

This is simply an example of what an average day of Eating Clean could look like. Feel free to conduct some research and adapt the meal plan. If you manage to complete 7 days of Eating Clean, once you get past the first few days of feeling groggy because your body is adjusting to a more balanced diet, you should begin to feel a lot more energetic, and a sense of peace and wellness should ensue. Do keep a diary comparing how you normally feel with how you feel after Eating Clean for one week.

Just to spice up your life a little bit, if you feel disciplined enough, you can include a 'Treat or Cheat day' once a week, where you can replace *one* of your meals with something of your choice, such as pizza, Chinese takeaway or a slice of red velvet cake. The chances are that your body will begin to like this type of food less and less, and it will no longer remain a staple in your diet. Choose wisely and enjoy a new blast of energy.

Sleep Matters

Since we have now covered physical exercise and Eating Clean, it is important to discuss sleep, as it is another key but often overlooked factor in maintaining good health. Research maintains that most healthy adults need on average 7-9 hours of sleep. In actuality, when examining the silent impact sleep has on my clients' levels of stress and anxiety, most maintain that they only average between 3-6 hours of sleep per night. This is because other things such as the internet, TV, socialising or working late have taken priority. As explored in the 'Autopilot' chapter, there is a cost to this.

Going to bed late and waking up early does not enable us to function at our best and feel a sense of peace and balance health wise. Going to bed and waking up early, however, may have more benefits than you think. The first is that you have given your body the ample room to rest and recuperate from all that the day has taken from you. I tend to be in bed by about 8:30pm and wake up at about 4:00am. I have found this to be most beneficial to pray, undertake a small amount of admin or work on the books I am writing, and exercise at home or at the gym before resuming my motherly duties at 7:00am, and counselling/pastoral/business duties at 9:00am. I have found this way of living to give me a spring in my step and a general feeling of being healthy. Committing to going to bed by 8:30pm the night before ensures that this is possible; otherwise, the tasks accomplished in the morning are unlikely to occur. Although this may feel like a sacrifice, I have found the benefits to be worth it. Has it required some active discipline and changes to be made in my daily habits? Of course! In being my own boss, it is often difficult to know when to cut off working. My husband and I made a pact recently not to check our phones for emails or social media after 6pm. This has gone a long way in bringing about a real sense of 'This is relaxation or winding down time', inducing a more peaceful feeling throughout our evening, as we prepare to engage in our 8 hours of night time sleep.

Generational Mindsets

If you are not used to a healthy way of living and haven't witnessed good examples of health in those around you, these changes are not ones that all individuals will find particularly easy. After taking our children to a funfair recently at a beach in Kent, we recognised that even though people know something is bad for them, it doesn't make it a given that they will change or stop that behaviour, even if it is affecting someone they love. In less than a 10-minute timeframe, we witnessed 7 pregnant mothers smoking a cigarette in the summer sun, whilst blowing the smoke in the vicinity of their other children, blissfully unbothered by the poison entering their little ones' lungs. In one case, there was a pregnant mother and a pregnant daughter engaging in exactly the same destructive behaviour. Smoking and alcohol misuse are clearly some of the hardest things to combat, but after witnessing clients and loved ones pass away from alcohol or smoking related diseases, there is always one common theme; they tend to wish that they had taken action sooner and that they hadn't allowed a simple 'bad habit' to take life, as they knew it, away from them. Take a moment to consider what type of mindset and behaviours you are passing down to your future generations, based simply on how they witness you treat your body and mind.

Me Time

"Me time?" I hear all the mums asking, "What on earth is that?" As tough as it is to take a moment to 'just be', as discussed in previous chapters, engaging in mindfulness or taking a 5-minute tranquil nature walk can help inject moments of peace into your daily happenings. It is important to take a few moments out of every day to just relax and take in the world around you. If you can schedule things like spa days in advance or a weekend trip in a peaceful environment with a loved one, this can go some way in helping you re-energise and face the week ahead.

Question Time

So, today, in your pursuit of peace in your health, what changes might you need to make? The following questions will allow you to take an inventory of where you are now, giving you the power to action plan for the future.

Current Status:

What is your height?

_____
_____

How much do you weigh?

_____
_____

Future Status:

Based on advice from your doctor/fitness research, are you considered to be the ideal weight for your height?

_____
_____

Do you have a goal weight or body type in mind?

_____
_____

If not, how much weight might you have to lose or gain to be considered more healthy?

_____
_____

Exercise:

1. Do you exercise in the week? If so, how often? (If 'No' go to question 5)

_____
_____

2. How much time do you allocate to each session?

_____
_____

3. Do you feel that this is sufficient to maintain good health? If not, could you commit to more?

_____
_____

4. What might need to change in your mindset/daily routine in order to achieve a better state of health? (Go to 'Diet' questions)

_____
_____

5. If you do not exercise, why not?

_____
_____

6. What type of benefits would there be to adding exercise to your regimen now?

_____
_____

7. What might you need to change in your daily routine in order to incorporate more physical activity?

_____
_____

Diet:

What does an average day of eating and drinking look like for you?

Breakfast

_____
_____

Snack

_____
_____

Lunch

_____
_____

Snack

_____
_____

Dinner

_____
_____

Snack

_____
_____

Is this way of eating sufficient to lead you to optimal health?

_____
_____

What unhealthy foods might you need to cut back on?

_____
_____

What healthy foods could you introduce?

_____
_____

What might be the benefits of eating a more balanced diet now?

_____
_____

Relaxation:

Do you take quiet moments?

_____
_____

What are some tranquil things you can introduce?

_____
_____

What small change can you make to introduce some more peace into your everyday routine?

_____
_____

When will you schedule your next nature walk, spa break or holiday?

_____
_____

What changes might you need to make to your sleeping habits and why?

_____
_____

Commitment:

Do you have a friend or family member who can commit to this journey with you?

_____
_____

If not, does this journey mean enough to you to go it alone?

_____

_____

What will making changes to your diet and health allow you to feel and do in the future?

_____

_____

What examples could you set for those around you?

_____

_____

If you have done everything you can to induce peace in your health, it will subsequently increase the probability that peace is easier to sustain in the other areas of your life. This is because if your health is out of order, it will be very difficult to focus on anything else. Is going on a health kick easy? No, but it is doable. Besides, within the first year of his liver transplant, Robert, who we talked about earlier, had climbed a mountain, did a 25-mile bike ride for charity, and exercises and Eats Clean every single day. If he can do it, what excuse do we have?

The Bible reminds us:

"Don't you realize that your body is the temple of the Holy Spirit, who lives in you and was given to you by God? You do not belong to yourself, for God bought you with a high price. So you must honor God with your body." (1 Corinthians 6:19-20, NLT).

Be healthy, be peaceful!

Love in Peace

Picture this: It's 11:15am, despite the forecast of rain, the weather is hot, the skies are blue, the water is crystal clear, and the sand is golden brown. My dress is made of lace; it elegantly falls just over the knee. I don't have a tiara because I am no longer that naïve, little 'princess', new to marriage and unaware of what lay ahead of her. I most certainly don't need a veil; he has already seen every inch of me, and stayed. The greatest gift a person can give you is acceptance, even after you have shown yourself undisguised. As I walk slowly along the brown planks of wood, hearing that familiar song from ten years prior, it prompts me to well up at the sanctity of this moment. I feel grateful for the sudden gush of wind, helping to stem the tears from falling and potentially destroying the masterpiece I had made of my face. As I approach the end of the stable walkway, I look towards the beach and pause for a moment, trying to fathom walking through this vast array of sand in five-inch silver peep-toe heels. Still, my love is waiting for me with the Minister at the edge of the seashore, so I wade through the sand, with each of my sons in hand, ready to recommit myself to their father, my friend, my love and my everything for the last seventeen years and beyond.

As I head towards him with the song *Make Me Whole* (by Amel Larrieux) still playing in the background, I watch intently as the cool breeze blows his white, short-sleeved shirt and beige trousers. Still, he stands firmly in his brown loafers, unmoved by the happenings of life. As the waves move back and forth, his hands are clasped behind his back as he awaits my arrival, much in the same way they were when we got married ten years before. I notice that familiar smile, an endearing look in the eyes, and feel assured that forever is still ours. After ten years and two children, we felt it important to renew our wedding vows amongst a handful of our closest family and friends on a beautiful stretch of Mexican beach. That day, we reminded each other and those around us that we 'still do'. The Minister said he preferred conducting vow renewals rather than marriage ceremonies, as still saying "I do" after walking through the reality of married life is not something that all couples are able to accomplish. As I looked into my husband's eyes that day, it was almost as though time stood still. I felt an overwhelming sense of peace, but this wasn't a new feeling. Despite all life has thrown at us over the years, the overriding feelings in our marriage were that of gratitude to God, togetherness and tranquility. With little or much, we would choose each other every time.

Celebrating ten years of marriage and seventeen years as a couple in their thirties may not feel like a massive accomplishment to everyone. However, being that neither of us witnessed how to sustain a loving, lasting and peaceful marriage, to us, this is most definitely a sizeable achievement. When thinking about how to go from pieces to peace in a relationship, there are a number of key points that came to mind. Although the scope of this book will not allow us to explore all of these ideas in depth, the book my husband and I penned together called *The Colours of Love Relationship Manual* highlights in minute detail how to create peace and harmony during the different stages of any relationship.

For the purposes of this book then, in reflecting on the numerous couples counselling sessions I have facilitated, as well as personal experience, there appears to be a key yet often overlooked component required for any relationship to flourish. Without this key component in place, many individuals describe a relationship that feels to be slowly crumbling. Put simply, it is the lack of a *felt sense* of support from one's partner that causes a once strong and sturdy relationship to begin falling to pieces. We will use the rest of this chapter to explore the significance of a perceived sense of support and how this can help you to experience love in peace.

Relationship Support

There are several definitions of the word 'Support'.

- The first is to Encourage, as in: To agree with and give encouragement to someone or something because you want him, her, or it to succeed: e.g. "My mother supported the Conservative Party all her life."
- Another definition of support is to Help, such as: To help someone emotionally or in a practical way: e.g. "Alcoholics Anonymous is a group that supports people who are trying to combat their dependency on alcohol."
- To Provide is an alternative definition of support. It means: To give a person the money they need in order to buy food and clothes and pay for somewhere to live: e.g. "He has a wife and four children to support."
- The final definition reads: To stop from falling, whereby you hold something firmly or carry its weight, especially from underneath: e.g. "When babies first learn to stand, they hold on to something to support themselves to stop themselves from falling." Isn't that what we all need at some stage of our lives? The assurance that the person we are in a relationship with will 'bear all or part of the weight', holding us up in times of weakness?

In the dictionary, regardless of the specific definition, the word 'Support' is always listed as a verb. From my recollection of Key Stage One English lessons in primary school, Mrs. Roberts always reminded us that a verb was a "doing word"; something that required "action". During several couples counselling sessions, I have often witnessed one partner defensively utter the words: "But I do support you! You know I do!" This in turn tends to be met with the other so-called 'wounded party' protesting that "Actions speak louder than words!" Many partners who feel 'unsupported' in their relationship have drawn this conclusion, simply because they haven't observed or experienced any actions from their loved ones that support the idea that they have someone who will bear all or part of the weight they are carrying. Subsequently, this feeling of being unsupported feeds into further beliefs about abandonment, loneliness and a lack of unity, consequently giving rise to the dissolution of peace.

The bearing all or part of the weight is essentially what I do in my role as a psychotherapist. I 'hold my clients up' and contain them when they feel unable to hold or contain themselves (Gray, 1994). This felt sense of 'presence' is enough to safely allow us to unpick difficult thoughts or events, which have been buried deeply in a dark and timeless place (Baldwin, 1987). Although my role is seldom solution focused, the notion of staying with someone whilst they battle feelings of depression, anxiety, hopelessness, guilt or shame is in and of itself 'healing' (Mearns & Thorne, 2000). The 'being there', 'holding up' and 'bearing the weight' rather than solving the problem itself is in fact what heals the soul.

The same can be said for romantic relationships, and as human beings, we have an innate ability to be there for the other in their suffering. A relationship is defined as: *The way in which two people are connected.* Connection without a felt sense of support is near impossible to attain, let alone maintain. If I begin to feel unsupported, the chances are that in time, I will begin to feel disconnected. The overriding but perhaps rarely verbalised question is: "Can I trust you to hold me up when my own legs are feeling wobbly?" If the likelihood of the answer to this question is a "no" or an "I'm not sure", thoughts of peace are likely to drift away in the same way an unmanned canoe would do so in the ocean. This type of uncertainty is crippling. It stops you from ever fully giving of yourself or ever fully exploring what could be.

A Felt Sense of Support

Since all definitions of support previously mentioned involved giving, helping and bearing weight, it must involve a reciprocal felt sense of interest, concern, focus and presence. With so many things vying for our attention, we must be mindful not to 'be there', without really 'being there'. In addition, it is important to seek clarity on what this felt sense of support would feel and look like in practical terms for your partner, thereby enabling you to accurately meet their needs. Only then does peace have a chance of making an appearance.

The Impact of Spiritual Support

As a pastor, I often engage in conversation with those alien or new to Christianity. Since bad things do happen in this world, their primary concern questions whether or not God can be trusted to hold their wobbly legs up in times of need. But the truth is, God never promised that we wouldn't have trouble. In fact, He forewarned us in John 16:33 (NIV) that

"In this world, you will have trouble. But take heart! I have overcome the world." Put simply, God is highlighting that in this life you lead, you will go through some difficult circumstances, but don't worry and try to remain positive, because when you do, I will be there and have already won the battle.

God is constantly reminding us through His Word that we can trust Him to support us during trying moments. Isaiah 43:2 (NIV) reads: *"When you pass through the waters, I will be with you; and when you pass through the rivers, they will not sweep over you. When you walk through the fire, you will not be burned; the flames will not set you ablaze."* In essence, when you go through bad things, I will be there, and what should destroy you, won't; I will be supporting you well enough to ensure that you come out on top. In the midst of this turmoil, Isaiah 41:10 (NIV) maintains: *"So do not fear, for I am with you; do not be dismayed, for I am your God. I will strengthen you and help you; I will uphold you with my righteous right hand."* We have spoken earlier in this book about peace and worry being unable to co-exist. God is saying here that because you have the support of my strong and invincible right hand, you can invite peace into your life and banish worry.

This support from God's unshakable right hand in part accounts for the following empirical research findings:

- Christians are more likely to cope better with stress and perceive it as less threatening (Antonovosky, 1967).
- Christianity is associated with lower levels of anxiety and depression, and as such, Christians are less likely to commit suicide, use drugs or become alcoholics (Abbotts et al., 2004;

Plante & Boaccini, 1997; Williams, 2003; Yarhaus et al., 2003, all as cited in Huckestein, 2008, p..33).
- Christians are capable of higher intellectual power, have a greater sense of purpose and responsibility for themselves and others, with the courage to face problems head on (Ellis, 2000, as cited in Huckestein, 2008, p..33).

These results bring to light the profound power of a perceived sense of support from God. It is this that allows many to feel like a *"tree planted by streams of water, which yields its fruit in season, and whose leaf does not wither, whatever they do prospers."* (Psalm 1:3, NIV). This subsequently allows you to calmly wait it out, quietly assured that He has enough strength to deposit within you during your period of weakness. If a perceived sense of support from an invisible God can produce this level of serenity, the possibilities are endless if we are also fortunate enough to receive this from a tangible human being inside a loving romantic relationship.

Support During Transition

So we have established thus far that a felt sense of support is pertinent to developing a peaceful environment with our significant other. Never has this rung so true as when one or both parties are embarking on a transition of any form. Transition refers to the process or a period of changing from one state or condition to another. Although change may be necessary, my clinical work and empirical research conducted suggests that it is seldom easy. Lebow (2006) maintains that there are five stages a given individual goes through before finally following through with a change of some type. This includes pre-contemplation, contemplation, preparation, action and maintenance. An individual will generally move through these stages many times until the transition is complete or abandoned midway. Take losing weight for example, as discussed in the previous chapter. Becoming healthier requires you to not only start, but also complete a process of change and transition from your usual routine. Even though slip-ups along the way are part and parcel of the process and provide opportunities for learning, as human beings, we tend to automatically internalise this as a sign of failure, encouraging subsequent hopelessness. It is in these times that a felt sense of support is key. Knowing that someone you love is rooting for you, even on something as simple (to some) as a weight loss journey, gives you the fuel you need to keep pressing on until you once again fit into those skinny jeans.

Throughout your relationship with your partner, you may go through many different types of transitions. These may be career related, geographical, financial, etc. The business world has now recognised that adaptation to change is difficult to manage within the workforce, hence why major financial organisations now employ individuals to specifically manage the process of change within the workplace. Their support is invaluable to the smooth operation of the organisation when both major and minor changes are implemented.

Our Relationship Transition

Early on in our relationship, my husband and I experienced a major transition that would change not only the trajectory of our lives but many people that would be affiliated with us then and in the future. My husband is now affectionately known as "Pastor G", but when I met him as a teenager, I believe that the title "Road G" would have been a little more befitting. Being "On Road" is an inner London colloquialism that essentially means the engaging in activities that are contrary to one that seeks to remain on the 'straight and narrow path'. Unbeknownst to us, a mere three months into our relationship, a near death experience would cause him to cry out to God to save his life, when the barrel of a smoking hot gun was held to his temple in the middle of a dark, black night. He vowed that if God saved him, he would serve Him. Sure enough, the same gun that had just been fired after him by 3 men in 'scream masks', as he ran frantically through the dark streets of South London alone, with bullets ricocheting off the wall, jammed right when the trigger of this loaded gun was pulled against his head. This for me has always been the ultimate credibility of God's power. Because my then partner chose life instead of death, and peace instead of possessions, a major transition *together* ensued.

My partner went from a life on the verge of criminality, with finances, fast cars and material goods at his disposal, to waiting at the bus stop and watching the 472 bus drive past and splash *us* in the pouring rain. I chose to highlight the word 'us', because we went through this extremely difficult transition, together. My support involved consistently reminding him through words and action that the promise over his life and potential he exhibited was far more appealing than any of the possessions he had chosen to let go of. Even so, this transition was not something either of us found particularly easy. We went from raving most weekends to every weekend, watching back to back episodes of Bishop T. D. Jakes preaching the word of God. Part of his transition from darkness to light required full immersion into the things of God, and a complete letting go of anything that was not of Him. Truth be told, although I knew that this transition was a positive one, sometimes, I was simply 'Jaked Out'! Jaked out or not, however, I would still sit there and watch it with him, as there was too much at stake to risk even a slight withdrawal of support.

The felt sense of support within our relationship was not one sided. My partner recognised that who I had met initially was not who he was becoming, and was patient and tender with me as we slowly worked things out. I realised that a felt sense of support as he finished his university degree, embarked on the corporate world of work, and began to lead mid-week Bible study ministries to help others affiliate with God's word would be necessary for our relationship to last the distance. For those difficult moments, I had to be the change we wanted to see and my grip on this relationship had to be stronger than the grip of what was calling him to go back into the fast life. However, it's not that my grip was stronger than his old life calling him back into a world of nothingness; it's just that mine had supernatural power behind it. In embarking on this drastic transition, we had to keep God at the centre of our relationship, because as Ecclesiastics 4:12 (CSB) maintains, *"A cord of three strands is not easily broken."* The peace we experience now in our relationship has a lot to do with this major transition we undertook, and the felt sense of support we provided each other during the process.

Practical tips for Support during Relationship Transition

If you are facing transition of any type in your relationship, perhaps an open and honest discussion about the following points may help bring about some much-needed clarity.

In your relationship, you may need to:

- Recognise if transition is necessary
- Talk about what the change will look like once it's complete
- Be honest about any fears or resistance to the change
- Discuss what type of support is required to help during the process
- Realistically consider what the main supporter feels they can offer and how the other partner could also offer support
- Talk about how the journey will be made a little easier on the supporter by the actions of the person who requires the support
- The end result may be favourable or it may not be, e.g. moving to a new dream job or one that simply pays the bills; how do you choose joy in the meantime?
- Set aside time to discuss things during the process, asking questions such as "What can I do better?"
- Once it is over, take an inventory of any achievements along the way and any areas of improvement
- Thank each other for the patience and sacrifice displayed along the way
- When you acknowledge and positively affirm each other, it makes one want to support the other more

Support During Loss

Thus far, we have examined the importance of support in regards to relationships, spirituality and transition. Before closing up this chapter, I believe it is lastly important to consider the significance of support during inevitable moments of loss, and how this can make room for peace during a period where it often feels to be unable to co-exist with despair.

In talking about peace within a relationship, one often greatly ignored factor in terms of support required is in the expansion of a family from 2 people to 3 or more. Welcoming a child into the world is generally seen as a beautiful thing, which it is, but it doesn't negate the potential for the felt support given by one's partner to be seen to dwindle. The transition from frequent and spontaneous date nights to breastfeeding, nappy changing and sheer exhaustion can be hard for a couple who have only ever focused on each other to adjust to. "Who is this new, tiny being that looks exactly like me, that everyone gushes over, that has my wife at his beck and call, that interrupts cuddle time and requires every last penny of my disposable income to spend on nappies and wipes?" This, my friend, is YOUR child. Having a baby indeed changes everything, and in order to have peace in the home, the provision of mutual emotional and practical support is key.

Our Story

Once my husband and I had gotten married, we had different timeframes in mind to have children. There is often this myth floating around that you will be able to conceive and deliver a child as and when you want to. Client work and the experiences of friends and family unfortunately tell a very different story. Fertility is not something to be taken for granted, and those of us who have been fortunate enough to hold our own baby in our own arms should be grateful.

After several honest and open conversations, my husband and I decided that 2 years into our marriage, once we had had a chance to first live simply as husband and wife, we would be open to trying for our first child. Unlike couples we know who have tried for several years to get pregnant to no avail, we were blessed enough to conceive within the first 2 months of trying. It was great; I had bought the baby journal, had already chosen a powerful Hebrew name, and was ready to continue on in this new journey towards motherhood.

Although we were unaware, early on in the pregnancy, miscarriage was imminent. Knowing something terrible is about to happen and feeling powerless to stop it is one of the most difficult things you could ever experience. This is heightened further when you know you serve a God who is powerful enough to turn this situation around, yet this time, He chooses not to. What do you do when you randomly open the Bible on scriptures that say *"I will even make a way in the wilderness, and rivers in the desert"* but the pregnancy hormone in your body is declining so fast that it suggests that this may not in fact be the case (Isaiah 43:19, KJV)? In hindsight, I believe that God was telling us that, as the start of this verse states, *"Behold, I will do a new thing."* But in those moments, we didn't want a new thing, we wanted 'this' thing. Isn't this where we often find ourselves? Unlike God, we are unable to see the consequences of our own desires, but oftentimes, we want it anyway. On reflection, my husband and I recognised that 'this' thing could have unfortunately led to sickness, further heartache or even death, but understandably so, this was a very difficult stance to assume during the process.

After hearing the bad news that a miscarriage was on the way, we both took time off work, laid in the bed together watching badly made movies that we could barely concentrate on, praying, singing and playing gospel music, in the hopes that God would turn this thing around. This was a time in our lives where we both felt at our weakest. As a spouse or partner of someone who is feeling weak, you can often feel helpless. It is in these times that we needed to pray each other through in order to help us navigate successfully this difficult season of our lives. The Bible talks about Christ sending His Holy Spirit to comfort and abide with us (John 14:16, KJV). I believe we also did this for each other through a word, a touch, a glance, a smile, or even a thumbs up. The Greek word, translated "Comforter" or "Counselor" (as found in John 14:16, KJV) is *parakletos*. This form of the word means: *One called to the side of another.* Being at the side of each other made this distasteful trial that much easier to stomach, enabling us to continue keeping our heads above the water.

Even though we asked God to change the negative prediction of the nurses, He didn't. I learnt that day that God is sovereign, and that He indeed sends *"rain on the just and the unjust alike"* (Matthew 5:45, NLT). Being Christians and pastors did not make us exempt from experiencing loss. Furthermore, we had to acknowledge that being that God is the alpha and omega (the beginning and the end), He knows why we had to walk through this agonising experience. In time, we were able to reconcile that, amongst many reasons, sometimes God allows you to go through things in order to help other people in the future. As pastors and as a psychotherapist, we feel a strong sense of empathy for the many couples we have encountered who have lost a child. Most significantly, sometime after this encounter, we had to pray for and support a couple who lost their second pregnancy, two years in a row on the first day of the year. We received the news of the tragedy at 2am, conducted a big, celebratory New Year's Day service in the morning, and went off in the afternoon to pray for a lifeless, beautiful, fully formed baby boy, and a room full of grieving family members. Being that God has blessed us with two children ever since, whilst grieving with them, we were somehow able to ignite hope in the midst of the tragedy, attesting to the fact that God does indeed restore the years that the locust devoured (Joel 2:25, NKJV).

Though the process of losing a child was one of the hardest things we have ever experienced, this was made easier by the support given to each other. We didn't deny ourselves or each other the chance to experience our truest, and at times ugliest, emotions. We recognised that although the woman physically miscarries the child, that, in actual fact, 'we' had miscarried together. We began a whole new faith journey together after this. One where we chose peace, togetherness, and refused to place the fears of what happened before onto these new pregnancies. We believed that God would hold these babies in the palms of His hands and that He would complete what He started (Philippians 1:6, NIV).

Conclusion

Although seldom talked about, support in a relationship therefore is a key component required for peace to thrive. One key thing to remember is: don't forget to support the supporter! As teammates, you need to ensure support is as reciprocal as it can be. Unreciprocated support can cause one to feel a lack of appreciation, perhaps resulting in a wavering of a willingness to provide continued support, eventually leading to relationship dissolution. Instead, search for and seize opportunities to be supportive in your relationship. Like in a nature documentary depicting wolves chasing elk through the snow, they could not secure a meal unless they supported each other in their efforts. Ecclesiastes 4:9-10 (NIV) reminds us that *"Two are better than one, because they have a good return for their labor: If either of them falls down, one can help the other up. But pity anyone who falls down and has no one to help them up."*

For peace in love, support, support, support!

Peace in Purpose

Purpose

In talking about peace in relation to one's career, although society has taught us to blindly seek to climb the career ladder, I believe it necessary to begin by discussing the concept of purpose. Purpose refers to: *The reason for which something is done or created, or for which something exists.* Everything ever created was done so with purpose in mind. For instance, even everyday items such as a pen is a purposeful creation. Its definition reads: *A pen is an instrument used to apply ink to a surface, usually paper, for writing or drawing.* Many books, speeches, songs, poems, visions or artistic drawings have been created using a pen. Martin Luther King's *"I Have a Dream"* speech was penned on a piece of paper, which encouraged civil rights laws to be passed. If that speech were never written, quality of life as we know it for ethnic minorities would have been very different. Yet, we seem to show a level of disregard for pens, misplacing them easily or nonchalantly pocketing them after paying in some money at the bank. Perhaps we show a lack of respect also for our purpose, simply because we do not really understand our value.

Sometimes I sit and ponder on what kind of world this would be if even the most basic items had not been created. Typewriters, for example, provided inspiration for other even more poignant items to evolve, such as the computer or subsequently, the smart phone. What if the world required you to find your purpose for it to function, more effectively and for someone else to find theirs? If so much thought went into the creation of these everyday items made by human hands, how much more thought did the supreme God give into creating you? Just like the pen referred to earlier, which is often perceived to be 'just a pen', there is a reason why God created you. Your job is to acknowledge that you were created with purpose in mind, seek out in what fashion you best function, and live this out, thereby creating a sense of peace in that you are finally aligned to your purpose.

"But I don't have a purpose!" I hear you attest. This is simply not true. The Bible says that everyone was born with a specific God-given purpose. Even before we were born, we were all created with a God-given purpose. Jeremiah 1:5 (MSG) states that *"Before I shaped you in the womb, I knew all about you. Before you saw the light of day, I had holy plans for you."* As such, everyone was born with gifts, talents and abilities to assist them in fulfilling their God-given purpose, which is outlined in Romans 11:29 (NLT): *"For God's gifts and His call can never be withdrawn."* However, it is the responsibility of each individual to learn his or her God-given purpose, as highlighted in the following verse: *"Don't copy the behavior and customs of this world, but let God transform you into a new person by changing the way you think. Then you will learn to know God's will for you, which is good and pleasing and perfect."* (Romans 12:2, NLT)

If you fail or refuse to learn your God-given purpose, your options automatically become: (a) your own personal vision for your life, (b) society's vision for your life, or (c) the devil's vision for your life. With these plans, you may experience great financial success. However, we must be mindful that all success is not *"good success"* as the bible reminds us in Joshua 1:8 (ESV). Contrary to popular belief, success is irrelevant to purpose and in the end, none of the visions listed above will bring you fulfillment, satisfaction or peace of mind and certainly do not ensure that you are walking in purpose. Proverbs 19:21 (NLT) reminds us: *"You can make many plans, but the Lord's purpose will prevail"*

Where's Wally?

"So how do I find my purpose?" I hear you ask. Do you remember the childhood book called *Where's Wally?* There would be a picture of hundreds of characters drawn on a page and your job would be to locate Wally. In order to find him, however, you would first need to first know what he looks like (he always wore glasses and a striped red and white hat!); the same is true for your purpose! There are many people that look like Wally, but are NOT Wally, just like your purpose. There are also so many other things in the picture, trying to grab your attention. You need to stay focused and find Wally, just like your purpose.

If you don't fuel your appetite for purpose, it opens the window for the following to occur in life:

- Taking any job
- Marrying any guy or girl
- Accepting any or all friendships
- Spending money frivolously without foresight
- Living a life without purpose, being unfulfilled in every part of your existence

Interestingly enough however, you don't actually *find* your purpose, you *learn* it! To *find* means to come upon, usually by accident, and God doesn't do accidents! Instead, in the same way you learn academic subjects, equally, you learn your purpose! God hid His purpose for your life deep within the recesses of your heart. Proverbs 20:5 (BBE) states that *"The purpose in the heart of a man is like deep water, but a man of good sense will get it out."* In order to draw His purpose out of your heart, you must be a man or woman of understanding. If you don't draw out your God-given purpose from deep within your heart, you will never learn it.

Proverbs 20:18 (MSG) goes on to highlight the way we learn our purpose. It says: *"Form your purpose by asking for counsel, then carry it out using all the help you can get."* Therefore, without proper counsel, you will not be able to learn your God-given purpose. You need to think very carefully, however, about whom you seek this counsel from. Careers Advisors, for instance, will not be able to tell you what your purpose is because they did not create or manufacture you. You need to go back to the operator's manual, which is the Bible, as it holds the blueprint of your life.

When clients come to see me as a psychotherapist, it's often because they need revelation of some type to help them move forward in their life. Although I do believe in the transformative power of working closely with a client in the therapeutic space, I do acknowledge my limitations as a fellow human being. Unlike Christ, I am human and cannot see into the future, nor did I create or purpose the individual in front of me. In Romans 8:27 (MSG), it states: *"He knows us far better than we know ourselves."* I believe our uncertainty would lessen if we utilised the unlimited access we have been granted to Him. Sometimes, individuals expect that in some capacity, *I* may be able to reveal the purpose of their existence. In actuality, I believe that as our creator, who has the unique ability to see and speak into our future, Jesus is the only one who can reveal His purpose for our lives, but if you don't spend enough time with Him, how will you ever find out? Matthew 7:7 (NLT) maintains that He will always answer you. Just spending time with God in his counsel allows you to continue everyday life in peace.

Let's Make a Start!

Simply, take a moment to ask God what your purpose is. He may answer you straight away or may reveal things to you slowly. In the meantime, think about and attempt to answer the following questions.

What are your gifts, talents and abilities?

_____

_____

_____

_____

Which of these are you most passionate about, and why?

_____

_____

_____

_____

Would you engage in using this gift frequently, even if you are not paid to use it?

_____
_____
_____
_____

If you were to fully utilise this gift, what impact could this have on those closest to you?

_____
_____
_____
_____

If you were to utilise this gift globally, what impact could this have on the world at large?

_____
_____
_____
_____

Have you ever worked or volunteered in a field that is related to this gift? If so, how?

If you are unable to use this gift on a grand scale at the moment, is there something you can engage in where you are able to use it on a smaller scale?

What might you need to have in place in order to use this gift on the scale you feel compelled to?

A Word of Caution

Although your answers to these questions may be useful for gaining clarity on the gifts and abilities given to you, God always wires you for your purpose, and these things may *be your purpose* or may be the thing that *leads* you to your purpose. As a child, teenager and adult, I was at one stage extremely passionate about songwriting, and believed that this is what I was called to do in this life. After wholeheartedly pursuing this for many years, I found that this ability to use words and melodies to touch the soul complemented the quiet ability God had placed inside me, which was the gift to reach those in need and renew their hope. I didn't ever think this character trait would be used on the scale it is now, within pastoring or in psychotherapy, because the examples I saw of pastors growing up was not something I felt able to live up to. Even when walking in purpose has felt financially burdensome, there is no greater feeling than knowing that you are doing exactly what God called you to do. Because we have done what He has asked us, indeed, we have never seen the righteous forsaken or seen them begging for bread (Psalm 37:25, NIV), because He has indeed supplied all of our needs, according to His riches in glory (Philippians 4:19, KJV).

One thing we have also learnt is that finding your purpose can sometimes be born out of a seemingly bad situation. My husband was made redundant from a role he believed he was having impact in. Unfortunately, although he was kind enough to listen to people's problems and try to find solutions to them, the targets involved in the role centred on placing them into employment, which he fell just short of. As such, his managers called him into a meeting with tears in their eyes about the prospect of letting him go. They knew he was a good worker, but evidently this is not where God had called him to be. Even though he was made redundant 5 months after having our first child, not one bill was missed, we went on a family holiday, and my husband penned his first book, *The F Word: Faith Is*. Through redundancy came purpose, the leap of faith for full-time pastoring, and never again working for another company or boss other than God.

This is what got us through the difficult times:

Psalm 23: 1-6 (TPT)

The Good Shepherd

"The Lord is my best friend and my shepherd. I always have more than enough. He offers a resting place for me in his luxurious love. His tracks take me to an oasis of peace, the quiet brook of bliss. That's where He restores and revives my life. He opens before me pathways to God's pleasure and leads me along in his footsteps of righteousness so that I can bring honor to His name. Lord, even when your path takes me through the valley of deepest darkness, fear will never conquer me, for you already have! You remain close to me and lead me through it all the way. Your authority is my strength and my peace. The comfort of your love takes away my fear. I'll never be lonely, for you are near. You become my delicious feast, even when my enemies dare to fight. You anoint me with the fragrance of your Holy Spirit; you give me all I can drink of you until my heart overflows. So why would I fear the future? For your goodness and love pursue me all the days of my life. Then afterward, when my life is through, I'll return to your glorious presence to be forever with you!"

So how do I know I have found my purpose and that my husband has found his? Because despite the challenges that prevail, we have fulfillment, satisfaction and peace of mind. The moral of this story then is that God may be taking you on the scenic route to revealing your purpose. Habakkuk 2:3 (AKJV) reminds us: *"For the vision is yet for an appointed time, but at the end, it shall speak, and not lie: though it tarry, wait for it; because it will surely come, it will not tarry."* Even if it seems to be taking a long time, don't become impatient and, like Esau in the Bible, give up your birthright, destiny or purpose for a bowl of beans. Stay close to God and you will find out what your purpose is in due course.

Don't Wait Until Tomorrow

Many of my clients talk about the things they would like to pursue in life, and 95% of them state that they will do this "tomorrow". As you can imagine, for many of these people, tomorrow becomes next week, next month and eventually, never. The Bible reminds us *"Whatever you do, do well. For when you go to the grave, there will be no work or planning or knowledge or wisdom."* (Ecclesiastes 9:10, NLT). In other words, once we pass away from this life there will be nothing else we will be able to pursue, thus we have to do it now with excellence, whilst we still have breath in our lungs. My cousin being murdered at 24 years old, one week before an offer letter from a major football club offered him a chance to pursue his purpose, is always enough of a reminder to me to not wait another moment.

The reason why many of my clients believe it is best to wait until tomorrow is because, truth be told, they don't actually buy into the idea that they have enough in them to do it today. Over the years, I have come to learn that self-belief is half the battle. In your pursuit of purpose, you need to take inventory of what and whom you have around you. I remember as a teenager being outside the exam hall and having to physically move away from people who spoke negatively about how they foresaw their ability in the upcoming exam. The timely affirmations from my mother of the simple phrase "You can do it, try again" allowed me to accomplish more than she could ever realise. Whenever her voice was absent, I had internalised it so much that in times of need, just like David in the Bible, I was able to encourage myself in the Lord, my God (1 Samuel 30:6, KJV). The same can be true for you. Tell yourself you can, back it up with action, rely on God for strength, and eventually, you will.

There is a well-known gospel singer called Israel Houghton who penned many soul-touching hits, reaching people from all walks of life with the love and grace of Jesus Christ. He once told a story of his mother wanting to abort him as a baby slowly growing in her tummy. If she had gone through with this abortion, the world would be void of his melodies of love, hope and restoration, and that would have been a terrible shame. If by some chance you were never born, what would your family, your community or the world have missed out on?

Above all, in regards to finding peace in your career, find Christ, then find your purpose, and pursue it with everything in you. You will never be at peace in your career if it isn't in line with your purpose. Find Christ, find purpose.

Financial Serenity

As we near the end of this book, having worked through ways to cultivate peace within yourself, your health, relationship and career, we are about to examine how to find peace in the area of your finances. The common saying 'Money makes the world go round', whether we like it or not, does have some truth to it. Money, or a lack there of, unfortunately accounts for many relationship and marriage breakdowns, a poor sense of wellbeing, and many families living on the breadline. This chapter will examine the difficulties inherent with mismanaged finances and will provide advice on how to move closer towards financial serenity.

Marlo's Story

Marlo was a 53-year-old father and husband who had found himself suffering from stress and recently began exhibiting behaviours symptomatic of depression. Marlo was a man's man and had always prided himself with being the breadwinner in his home. Despite 30 years of service with this company, liquidation was imminent, and it was unlikely his redundancy settlement would suffice. Marlo found himself unsure of how he would continue to support his family, due to the underlying ageism he felt would prevent him from securing further employment. In Marlo's mind, being made redundant from such a longstanding and reputable firm was never something *he* would have to encounter. As such, he never thought to put anything aside for a rainy day.

During our counselling sessions together, he highlighted the unbearable thought of disappointing his family, due to his new inability to provide for them. This led to questions about his self-worth as a man and subsequently, thoughts of suicide began to emerge. The only reason Marlo was able to dispel thoughts of taking his own life was because he had failed to invest in life insurance or a funeral plan, and couldn't bear to have been a further burden even in death; something he could never undo.

If you consider that the source of Marlo's unrest is a *potential* future lack of finances, his response to it may sound extreme. Unfortunately, however, I witness this type of thinking quite frequently in many clients from all walks of life. They tend to equate their value with the amount of capital they have accumulated, and as such, their confidence is buried in their credit cards, fast cars and designer goods. These types of individuals tend to engage in a very self-destructive cycle. If they have money, they feel good; if they don't, they feel bad. Consequently they borrow more money, ignoring rising interest rates, in order to feel good again, if only for a moment. When the errors of their ways finally catch up with them, they find themselves in a deep, dark pit, unsure and unable to get out of it, and very far from a feeling of peace.

When I think about the curriculum taught in UK schools, I recognise that although we spend a vast amount of time learning mathematical concepts such as algebra, seldom do we cover the life skills required to effectively manage money. At 16 years old, we are all eligible to apply for that National Insurance card and embark on our very first job. Unless sound money management values were taught in the home however, it is likely that one will spend the money even quicker than one received it. In order to go from pieces to peace in your finances, it is important to take a frank look at your money management track record to date. Finding financial freedom or accumulating wealth is unlikely to occur if we don't know how to manage the little we have in the first instance. The Bible says that *"whoever can be trusted with very little can also be trusted with much."* (Luke 16:10, NIV). Before we explore this, it is necessary to uncover some financial insight that may help to shift your thinking to encourage better money management, not only for you, but also for your generations to come.

Money Myths

If a one-year-old child were to look at a £10 note, it may simply appear in their eyes to be a piece of paper with little to no value. They are blissfully unaware that money is in fact the very medium of exchange that allows for their nappies and food to be bought, and essentially keeps a roof over their heads. The burning question for most however in regards to money is how you accumulate more of it, and how you keep more of what you already have, thereby creating a sense of peace as it pertains to your pocket.

There are several myths about money, especially in the Christian community, where the general depiction is overwhelmingly negative. Money however is nebulous, and it can be used for good or evil, depending on whose hand it is in and the mindset behind it. For instance, £10,000 could be used to feed starving children across the world. Equally, the same £10,000 could be used to strike arms deals and incite acts of terrorism or war. Biblically speaking, however, 1Timothy 6:10 (KJV) outlines that it is the *love* of money that is the *"root of all kinds of evil"*. In chasing money, this verse highlights that some people have wandered from the faith and pierced themselves with many griefs. As with anything, there should be nothing we chase more than God, especially since contrary to popular belief, money in and of itself is powerless to solve all of life's problems. If it could, wealthy clients seeking peace would not make up 75% of my client base.

Ultimately, I have found the Bible to be true in that God does supply all of our needs. Matthew 6:31-33 (ESV) says: *"Therefore do not be anxious, saying, 'What shall we eat?' or 'What shall we drink?' or 'What shall we wear?' For the Gentiles seek after all these things, and your heavenly Father knows that you need them all. But seek first the kingdom of God and his righteousness, and all these things will be added to you."* Deuteronomy 8:18 (NIV) reminds us: *"But remember the LORD your God, for it is He who gives you the ability to produce wealth, and so confirms his covenant, which He swore to your ancestors, as it is today."* Knowing and believing these two verses, when it comes to finances, surely we should all feel at peace.

Financially Free?

It is apparent therefore that we all have this power to accumulate wealth. The question however pertains to whether we also have the required strategies to see it manifest. In order to keep more of what we earn, we must first become financially free. Financial freedom in this context does not refer to becoming filthy rich. Rather, it is a foundational step that relates to sensibly managing income and expenditure, thereby allowing you to comfortably meet your family's needs. In turn, this encourages the actualisation of the biblical concept of lending rather than borrowing, and thus, makes room for financial peace to thrive (Deuteronomy 28:12, NKJV). In contrast, being financially bound includes:

Having expenditure outweigh income: Whenever you have less money coming in than you do going out, you will always be working from a deficit or a place of weakness, rather than a place of strength. Unless care is taken to either increase income or decrease expenditure, it is probable that one will begin to borrow money in order to meet their basic expenses. If this pattern continues on, debt is likely to increase, casting a dark shadow on your ability to ever soar on your own.

Debt accumulation: Not all debt is bad. Take a house, for instance: in London, depending on the area, the average house costs anywhere in the region upwards of £400,000. If for instance you and your spouse had a combined annual salary of £50,000, without an inheritance or intentional saving for many years prior, it is unlikely that the average couple will be able to purchase such a house with cash. As an alternative, most couples apply for a mortgage. In many cases, the lender requires you to have saved up enough of a deposit to invest into the property also. On balance, houses are often seen as appreciating rather than depreciating assets; something that will make you a profit in the future or that can be passed on through future generations. Cars, in contrast, are generally depreciating assets. At best they will hold their value after a few years, and are therefore not purchases that will benefit you in the long run. This notion has contributed to the rise in leasing cars where customers opt to trade their car in for a newer version after a 3-year period, for example.

Deciding to apply for credit for non-essential everyday or designer items with extortionate and unmanageable interest rates is a questionable financial decision that may provide momentary euphoria, but seldom provides a peace that lasts. Unlike our God, who will *"forgive their iniquities and remember their sins no more"* (Hebrews 8:12, NIV), credit agencies operate in a slightly different fashion. Instead, they keep accurate records of your money mismanagement to date, which is often held against you when you need to make important future purchases on credit. Periodically obtaining and analysing your credit report is important to improve your financial standing and to correct any anomalies. The bottom line is that accumulating debt without a sufficient plan in place to combat it often leads to a host of other detrimental, yet avoidable problems, pushing you further and further away from a sense of peace within your finances.

When some individuals have exhausted all possibilities of applying for formal credit, their consumerist attitude to money leads them down the slippery slope of borrowing money from friends and family. As this vicious cycle of borrowing continues, their sense of financial independence diminishes alongside their peace.

Having a lack of savings: Proverbs 13:11 (NIV) says, *"whoever gathers money little by little makes it grow"*. Ensuring that you have accumulated enough savings is one way to feel at peace within your finances. You don't have to put a large amount aside each month, but in this case, putting something aside is certainly better than nothing. Since rainy days rarely announce their impending arrival, having money set aside is good foresight. Financial strain during unexpected tragedies can also be an additional source of frustration, so planning in advance for those 'just in case' moments in life can allow an otherwise difficult situation to be a little easier to manage.

Benefits of Financial Freedom

Because there are so many disadvantages to remaining financially bound, it is important to explore exactly how to become financially free. Before doing so, we must acknowledge a few of the many benefits of financial freedom:

Financial freedom provides stability: Whenever a household lacks the money they require to function properly, instability and uncertainty will surround their living situation. From working with many homeless people, who were once doctors, lawyers or CEOs of major companies, I have come to learn that we are all simply one pay cheque away from ever experiencing the same fate. Having a good amount of savings or sound investments allows for a sense of stability, which helps to induce peace, should the worse happen.

Financial freedom allows independence: Attaining financial freedom does not leave you at the mercy of others in the same way as being financially bound does. Complete financial autonomy allows you to work when necessary and also reward yourself with a well-earned break when needed. Moreover, you can make important beneficial financial decisions without having to rely on others to subsidise the cost.

Financial freedom provides opportunities to impact society and help the needy: Financial freedom can empower you to empower others. If you begin thinking beyond yourself and your generation, you can invest in the futures of those who will lead our world in time to come. For example, you could influence the world for good by setting up schools, which push empowerment and life skills or biblical principles to ensure they achieve *"good success"* (Joshua 1:8, KJV) in the future. This type of thinking also allows you to be a practical blessing to those from impoverished backgrounds, needing a hand up rather than a handout.

Financial freedom gives you access to the best of everything: On a personal level, being financially free can allow you and your loved ones to have access to the best housing, health and education systems. Imagine how much more opportunity could be granted to us if money were no object? We all know that money cannot buy peace, however, enough of it can help to eliminate a few extra problems.

Financial freedom allows you to be an active Kingdom Partner: When thinking beyond the self, being financially free allows us to partner financially to support the expansion of God's Kingdom (supporting Christian projects). I watched a documentary recently where the Saudi royal family was on a mission to invest heavily in Islam, funding the most lavish mosques and Islamic agendas, all in the hopes of having more people convert to their way of being. From pastoring a church in London, I do often find myself wishing that more Christians engaged in the same type of thinking, and were diligent about the biblical principle of tithing, which states that we should give a tenth (before tax) of what God has given us the ability to earn, back to the work of His Kingdom.

Tithing used to be a hard principle to grapple with, as I once believed that *my* money was *my* money. On reflection however, I recognised that if He didn't wake me up in the morning, keep me fit and healthy, provide me with food to eat, and the job in the first instance, I would not be able to go to work and earn the money. In beginning to adhere to Malachi 3:10 (NIV), *"Bring the whole tithe into the storehouse, that there may be food in my house. Test me in this,"* says the LORD Almighty, *"and see if I will not throw open the floodgates of heaven and pour out so much blessing that there will not be room enough to store it"*, I have found that He does indeed care for those who are obedient. For example, just recently, we undertook some home improvements inside our property. The final bill was over double the original quote and we were a little concerned as to how to make up the shortfall without dipping into our savings. We made a joke a week prior about not receiving a tax rebate for a few years, and low and behold, our accountant notifies us of a tax rebate due to us for over the amount required to pay the refurbishment bill. The first thing we did from that rebate was not to pay the refurbishment; instead, we opted to tithe to say thank you to God for His provision in our time of need. It would be untrue for me to suggest that tithing always results in a monetary blessing, because it doesn't. However, I have come to experience constant blessings from God in many different areas of my life, which I attribute in part to obedience to His commands. Adhering to the tithing principle simply demonstrates that in our lives, money is not greater than God. The remaining 90% for those who tithe seems to stretch further, so much so that they are seldom in worry or need, and when they are, they can simply remind God of the provisions He promised in Malachi 3:10. Furthermore, we need to move away from the urge to only desire the blessings of God, but refuse to acknowledge any part of His commands that requires active participation or sacrifice on our part. Just like in any loving human relationship, reciprocity and honour is key.

A quote from Proverbs 11:24-26 (MSG) reads: *"The world of the generous gets larger and larger; the world of the stingy gets smaller and smaller."* Unfortunately, much like my previous primitive thinking, for many reasons there sometimes appears to be an underlying reluctance for people to give a small portion of their finances over to the church. If all of our hearts broke for the things that break God's heart, the church would be in a position of strength, better able to meet the needs of others, as per the mandate left by Jesus Christ. Many churches are registered as charities, yet their hands are tied when the people who consume from the church on a weekly basis are themselves tight fisted and refuse to give back. My prayer is that we don't continue to groom a generation of Christians who resemble the rich, young ruler (Mark 10:17-27, NLT); happy to do everything for Christ except give up their money to the poor, despite their awareness that this was the gateway to Heaven. The Bible has asked us to *"go into all the world to preach the gospel"* (Mark 16:15, NIV) and reminds us that Jesus has come to seek and save those who are lost. I do hope that we get to a place where we don't mind handing over money to help build God's agenda, in the same way we freely hand it over to McDonald's, who give us nothing of substance in return.

Multiple Streams of Income

Now that we have considered the benefits of becoming financially free, this paragraph considers a method of accumulating more wealth than you currently have at present. Wealth accumulation is unlikely to occur via working a standard 9-5 job, where you are just about making ends meet. Over the years, we have found that using our gifts and talents, such as Key Note Speaking, Songwriting, Authoring, Mentoring, etc., has allowed us to generate 80% more income than we would be able to by only relying on one source of income generation. For some people, this may involve cake baking, football coaching or clothes alterations, etc. In addition, it is important to be proactive in terms of working towards promotion or seeking better benefits/income in the hopes of being more financially secure. Always consider how much value is placed on the work you undertake and realistically, whether your pay reflects this, making appropriate adjustments accordingly. Take a moment to consider how you and your family can generate multiple streams of income.

Financial freedom therefore has the potential to solve a variety of issues for yourself and for mankind, bringing about a sense of peace in your home, your community, and in your generations to come. The next part of this chapter will help you take an inventory of your current financial thinking and prompt you to make the changes necessary to find peace in this area of your life.

Financial Goals

In attempting to become financially free and at peace with your finances, it is important to first set some financial goals. Exercise 1 helps you to set some financial goals over various timeframes. Be both honest and realistic about what is attainable, considering your current status, so to avoid setting yourself up to fail.

Exercise 1: Financial Goals

What are 3 financial goals you would like to achieve in the next 6 months? (e.g. to save a certain amount, to clear a specific amount of debt etc.)

1. _____

2. _____

3. _____

What are 3 financial goals you would like to achieve in the next year?

1. _____

2. _____

3. _____

What are 3 financial goals you would like to achieve in the next 5 years?

1. _____

2. _____

3. _____

What are 3 financial goals you would like to achieve in the next 15 years?

1. _____

2. _____

3. _____

My Current Attitude to Money

In order to reach these financial goals, it's important to look at your current attitude to money. Exercise 2 looks at your thoughts around finances.

Exercise 2: My Attitude to Money

Please rate your thoughts about money from 1 (Strongly Disagree) to 5 (Strongly Agree):

Statement No.	Statement	Agreement Level 1-5
1.	Money is for spending	
2.	Money is for saving/investing	
3.	I give money to charity	
4.	I believe in and adhere to the	

		principle of tithing	
5.		My financial priorities are being cared for	
6.		It is important to live on a budget	
7.		My money is my money to use as I see fit	
8.		It is acceptable to borrow money to have the finer things in life	
9.		It is acceptable to borrow money to manage an unexpected financial crisis	
10.		I would be happy to ask for financial support from my friends or family	
11.		If I got into financial difficultly, I would be happy to cut back on expenditure	
12.		I believe and adhere to the principle of making financial plans for my future	
13.		In a marriage, I would be comfortable managing the family finances	
14.		If I couldn't afford something, I would wait until I could	

15.	If I couldn't afford something, I would find a way to get it regardless	
16.	Being in debt is normal and acceptable	
17.	Not paying off a debt, even when I have the money to pay towards it, is acceptable	
18.	I keep an eye on my credit file	
19.	Generally speaking, I have enough money to accommodate my lifestyle	
20.	I am in a position and would be willing to help a family member or friend financially if they were in need	
21.	I am happy to use some of my money to further God's Kingdom	
22.	The amount of money I have dictates whether I am happy or sad	
23.	If I came into a large sum of money, I would buy everything I have ever wanted	
24.	It is likely I will rent a home for the rest of my life	
25.	It is likely I will own a home	

	outright in my lifetime	
26.	My credit file speaks well of my money management skills	
27.	It is possible that Bailiffs may visit my premises at some point during my lifetime	
28.	My current attitude to money is one I believe would be beneficial to pass down to my children	
29.	I have set aside money for funeral plans or have life insurance in place	
30.	My current attitude to money means 3 generations ahead will be financially secure	

After completing Exercise 2, how likely is it that the goals set above will become a reality with your current attitude to money? Is a shift in your thinking required?

_____
_____
_____
_____
_____
_____
_____

My Current Money Management Style

Your attitude to money impacts exactly how you manage it and how much peace you have with it. Exercise 3 takes inventory of how you spend your money.

Exercise 3: My Spending Habits

Please estimate the percentages of your monthly salary that you spend on the following (the total must add up to 100%):

Expense/Item	Percentage of Salary Allocated Towards This (e.g. Mortgage 47%)
Mortgage/Rent	
Bills (Electric, Water, Council Tax, etc.)	
Food Shopping	
Car (Hire Purchase, Petrol, Insurance)	
Total Household Contribution (if you live with parents)	
Travel	
Saving	
Tithes and Offerings	
Investment	

Eating Out	
Leisure Activities	
Purchasing Shoes, Clothing, Cosmetics	
Holidays	
Children's Activities/Expenses	
Other_____	
Other_____	
Other_____	
Other_____	

What might you need to change, if anything?

_____
_____
_____
_____
_____
_____
_____

Learning to Budget

Luke 14:28 (NIV) says: *"Suppose one of you wants to build a tower. Won't you first sit down and estimate the cost to see if you have enough money to complete it?"*

Unfortunately, we don't always count the true cost of embarking on something new financially before we sign on the dotted line. This seldom ends well. As mentioned earlier on in this chapter, there is no guidance given on how to manage money within our education system. Money management skills for me came directly from my mother, who taught us the importance of differentiating between needs and wants, and also taught us how to set and live on a budget. She deterred us from buying anything on credit, but rather to save up our finances in order to purchase what we needed in the future. This has gone a long way in ensuring my own household is financially secure, and these are the same principles we are instilling in our children's future generations, thereby creating a sense of peace, rather than the usual anxiety when it comes to money.

A Hard Lesson Learned

I remember being a young adult, living at home with my family, working full time with minimal outgoings but still having no money. It seemed I had moved away from the sound principles given by my mother and was bearing the consequences. It became clear that future goals of owning a home, going on holiday at will, investing or having a sizeable amount of savings would not materialise if I didn't make some immediate changes. I decided to create my own strategy of budgeting, by way of a Finance Sheet in Microsoft Excel, which helped me account for all income and expenditure in real time. The spreadsheet was simple; it contained details of monthly wages and financial responsibilities, and used formulas to automatically calculate disposable income. It required disciplined daily or bi-weekly updating of expenditure, but over the years, has afforded us the luxury of never being in the red, and being able to keep hold of and sensibly enjoy more of what we work hard to earn.

Exercise 4: Living on a Budget

Although there are many smartphone apps available to help with budgeting, I have found this method to continue to suffice for my financial accounting needs. Below is an example of the layout of a Finance Sheet you may wish to re-create in a programme like Microsoft Excel to help manage your finances. Formulas will be required to automatically calculate your disposable income each time you spend.

Feel free to use the paper version in the first instance to help paint a picture of how best you can manage your finances.

Rachel Smith's Finance Sheet Example

Date	Income (e.g. Monthly wage amount after tax)	Bill/Expense	Amount	Total Expenditure	Disposable Income
1.4.18	£1754.23	Tithe	£200.00	£1594.54	£159.69
		First Fruits/Offering	£30.00		
		Mortgage	£542.57		
		Council Tax	£148.00		
		Savings	£100.00		
		Food Shopping	£150.00		
		Water	£36.00		
		Electricity	£51.00		
		Car Insurance	£56.98		
		Travel	£104.00		
		Petrol	£50.00		
		Sky	£36.00		
		O2	£39.99		
		Date Night	£50.00		

My Finance Sheet

Date	Income (e.g. Monthly wage amount after tax)	Bill/Expense	Amnt	Paid? (Mark 'Yes' in Excel after checking bank statement)	Total Expend	Disposable Income

Instructions:

- Please list all your bills/expenses

- Please use estimates if you do not have exact amounts
- Use a calculator to tally these up
- How much disposable income do you have left?

With the actual Finance Sheet you create in Microsoft Excel, you will need to:

- Update it every time you spend from your account
- Frequently analyse your online banking statement every few days to ensure accuracy
- Type 'Yes' in the 'Paid' column when a bill has actually been debited from your bank account
- Regularly email yourself an update of your finance sheet which will provide an accurate picture of your disposable income
- Do not spend outside of this disposable amount and budget sensibly for the remaining duration of the month

Goal Adjustment

Based on the new information from Exercise 4, do your goals need adjusting?

Is there some new thinking required around the goals set when you consider your budget and saving capacity? For example, if buying a house in 5 years was the goal, is it possible that it could be done in 1 year if the location changed to outside London or if you used a Government Home Ownership Scheme as a stepping stone? What are the pros and cons to making such adjustments?

What Am I Thinking?

In adjusting these goals, it's important to take a frank look at your thinking when it comes to finances. For example:

- How aware am I of the benefits finding true financial freedom could provide for my lifestyle?
- How important is it to me to become financially free?
- Am I thinking "Council flat or owned home"?
- Am I thinking "Buy for now or build for the next 3 generations"?
- Am I thinking "I must attend all birthday dinners costing £40 per head" or "I need to save this money for my future"?

The truth of the matter is that what you are exposed to is what you will become like, which will in turn determine how much peace you have in your finances. Consider therefore reflecting on the subconscious messages about finances you were exposed to as you grew up. In the inner city London community I grew up in, whenever someone came into money, they bought designer clothing, such as the 'Moschino Cats and Dogs suit' which was very loud, could only be worn within that fashion season, and certainly didn't last from the multiple washes at the broken down launderette. In some other communities, in contrast, when they come into wealth, rather than spending it on lavish items of clothing, they first put money aside and invested in appreciating assets like property. What kind of thinking are you engaged in, and what type of thinking will you subsequently pass down to your future generations?

The Accumulation of Wealth

In putting all of the principles above into practice, in time, you should find yourself in a better financial position. Let's assume that in adhering to these principles, you have now accumulated £500,000 to use as you please. Hypothetically speaking, this amount is not something you won from the National Lottery; you, my dear, have earned this £500,000 yourself. In this final exercise, break down to the penny what exactly you would do with this money to ensure peace within your finances for the future to come.

Exercise 5: My £500,000

Please estimate exactly what you would do with the £500,000 that you have earned by managing your finances correctly.

Expense/Item	Amount

Once you have finished, consider whether with this plan, you have included some or all of the following:

- Have you bought somewhere to live, paid for with cash or mortgaged?
- Have you tithed to God?
- Have you put some of the finances aside in savings?
- Have you set aside an inheritance for your children/grandchildren?
- Have you cleared any debts?
- Have you provided financial support for your parents?
- Have you made sensible financial investments?
- Have you donated money to charity or those in need?
- How much have you allocated for disposable income?

Accumulating wealth can be the answer to many problems, but without exercising wisdom and strategies, keeping hold of it will be extremely difficult. For example, there are a vast number of lottery winners who don't know how to properly manage their money. As a result, they spend it lavishly and within a few years, wind up more broke than they were to start with. What you do with wealth once you obtain it will be determined by what you did with it before you were financially free, your new attitude to money, and whether your thinking transcends the now. Ecclesiastes 7:12 (NIV) says *"Wisdom is a shelter as money is a shelter, but the advantage of knowledge is this: Wisdom preserves those who have it."* Apply wisdom to your finances and preserve it.

Before closing this chapter, however, I believe a word of caution is necessary: Matthew 6:24 (NIV) says, *"No one can serve two masters. Either you will hate the one and love the other, or you will be devoted to the one and despise the other. You cannot serve both God and money."* Whilst it is noble to endeavour to become financially free, never put your finances in the place of God. Matthew 6:19-20 (TPT) reminds us: *"Don't keep hoarding for yourselves earthly treasures that can be stolen by thieves. Material wealth eventually rusts, decays, and loses its value. Instead, stockpile heavenly treasures for yourselves that cannot be stolen and will never rust, decay, or lose their value. For your heart will always pursue what you value as your treasure."* Since God has *"many mansions"* stored up for us in Heaven (John 14:2, KJV), He really should be treasure enough, especially being that *"we brought nothing into this world, and it is certain we can carry nothing out"*, including our finances, which are of no value in the grave (1 Timothy 6:7, KJV). Ultimately, making better financial decisions and always seeking God first will leave you richer in peace than you can ever imagine.

The Invitation

As we draw close to the end of this book, I believe this is a prime time to look back over our shoulder and take inventory of what we have covered. In summary, we have explored in great detail our pursuit for peace and the impact our thoughts, feelings, unexpected drama and our start in life can have on it. The main crux of this book utilised biblical, psychotherapeutic, and practical examples and techniques to enable us to cultivate more peace in 5 key areas of our life. Before leaving you to mull over all of this information in the hopes of putting it into action, I feel compelled to leave you in the same way that I started, with a client story. Particularly befitting is also the notion of granting you with an explicit invitation to become more deeply acquainted with this particular 'source bigger than life itself' which I mentioned in the introduction; the driving force behind many of my clients, as well as myself, truly journeying from pieces to peace.

Ronald's Story

My client, Ronald, was a 21-year-old student, still battling with the guilt and shame associated with a failed suicide attempt 5 years prior. He had been subjected to constant bullying and isolation at school, and fleeting ill-thought-out words from his mother, telling him to "Get out of my sight" had been the nail in the coffin. Her words, whether she meant them or not, had pushed him over the edge, making it easier for him to act on his thoughts of taking his own life. As his unguarded mind allowed his thoughts to indeed become his actions, he woke up early in the morning to set his plan into motion. After taking 14 different types of pills and downing a dangerous cocktail of strong alcoholic beverages, Ronald became unconscious on the floor at home alone, awaiting his fate. His dad, who was usually at work at this time, uncharacteristically came home early. He found Ronald with moments to spare and sought the medical care required to keep him alive. After the incident, there were many words left unsaid. It had become a taboo subject within the home, seemingly dead and buried in the eyes of his family, but every much alive within him today.

"Why do you think you lived?" I asked him. "What do you mean?" he said, with a puzzled look on his face. I paused and collected my thoughts before proceeding with my next question. "You took 14 different types of pills and drank dangerous amounts of alcohol in the hope of leaving this world; why do you think it didn't work?" "I don't know, but if you are eluding to some type of higher power, I don't believe in any of that type of stuff. I just think it was biological. I didn't take enough pills and alcohol to kill me."

During 12 sessions of working through the difficulties associated with a failed suicide attempt with Ronald, it became evident that the effects of his choices in his moment of despair had robbed him of peace long-term. Ronald was riddled with guilt, shame and unforgiveness in his heart for those who contributed to him wanting to end his life, and ultimately himself for attempting to commit suicide in the first place. Five years after the event, his past still had him and had thrust him into a life of hopelessness and depression. Although I know that not all clients believe in the existence of the spiritual realm (and nor would I force this belief on them), I remember thinking that if he did in fact believe in the higher power I did, he would have a remedy for his pain. Micah 7:18-19 (MSG) outlines this clearly:

"Where is the god who can compare with you, wiping the slate clean of guilt, Turning a blind eye, a deaf ear, to the past sins of your purged and precious people? You don't nurse your anger and don't stay angry long, for mercy is your specialty. That's what you love most. And compassion is on its way to us. You'll stamp out our wrongdoing. You'll sink our sins to the bottom of the ocean."

If you haven't noticed already, the common thread throughout this book, as highlighted at the start, is the need for a *combination* of practical, psychotherapeutic and biblical tools to help you with your pursuit of peace. Although Ronald and I did make some headway with his failed suicide attempt, I believe that true and complete healing for him will remain out of his reach until he reacquaints himself with the tender, loving mercies of the God who created him. For people that are alien or new to Christianity, I felt it necessary before we close to explicitly explain how my journey with getting to know Christ for myself has not been a smooth one. I even believe there are some special reminders in here for those who have that 'oh so special seat' in the church pew. Although Christianity has been instrumental with helping many clients and myself in our pursuit of peace, contrary to popular belief, I haven't had to be perfect in order to travel on this dusty road to get to know my creator, and neither do you.

My Story

"No makeup, check, no jewellery, check, no watching TV on Sabbath, check, appearing 'Godly', check, having a real relationship with Jesus Christ, uncheck."

This was much of my reality in relating to God during my formative years. I had developed a type of Godliness, never really believing that His power could actually change me. I had learnt how to look like a 'good Christian', not recognising however that there was in fact no such thing.

Although not all Christian denominations require this level of immersion, the Christian denomination I had grown up in became a major part of my everyday existence. It informed education, relationship and lifestyle choices, even down to the food on the dinner table. At age 4, it propelled my family into a life of soya milk, mock duck, tofu and red lentils. Vegetarianism had become our new way of being, whilst we endured the ridicule from our wider meat-eating family, who could not comprehend our sudden aversion to eating animals. Church was where I formed core friendships, went on quarterly camping expeditions, and developed talents such as performing arts and songwriting. Additionally, it was like a safe haven, protecting some of us from falling victim to the snares of our local community, which called us into a life of nothingness, teenage pregnancy at best or, at worst, drug taking or dealing. We became well versed in what we were forbidden to partake in, and had internalised an elitist attitude that Sabbath keepers would be the only ones to make it into Heaven. If however you had real problems, needed to demonstrate faith in action, or generate a sense of peace in dire circumstances, this was not the place for you.

This type of Christianity had become the yardstick by which I measured myself and others to be either good or bad, or saved or unsaved. As time progressed, that same stick and measurements I applied to others were also felt to be implicitly applied to me at church, depending on whether or not my skirt was the right shade of white. This subsequently began to mirror my perception of God. Rather than looking to Him as a loving, caring and all accepting father who only wanted the best for me, I looked at Him as a tyrant God, ever ready to condemn me when I fell short of His unattainable expectations. As you can imagine, I seemingly had God, but I had no peace.

Whilst I am very grateful for the foundation and principled living growing up within this denomination gave me, it took me leaving this denomination at aged 16 to unlearn all the rules and regulations imparted within me in an attempt to start again in my pursuit of peace. From excelling in Religious Education at GCSE level, I had acquired great insight into other religions and what they had on offer. It appeared however that each required me to be on a path to perfection in my own human strength, in order to reach God/peace. In my re-learning of Christianity, I began to recognise that put simply, God really loves us and desires to be close to us, like a father is with his child. All Christ required was for me to 'come to Him' and He would take care of the rest.

In studying deeper, it became clear that unlike any of the other figureheads in other religions, Jesus Christ had made the ultimate sacrifice by giving up His life for all the sins that I would ever commit in the future so I could be in a relationship with Him. In the Old Testament in the Bible, because of the sin committed by Adam and Eve, there was a barrier or a veil between God and man. The only way we could access God was once a year and through the High Priest on Yom Kippur, the Jewish solemn holy day, known as The Day of Atonement (Leviticus 16, NIV). Every year, the High Priest had to perform rituals to atone for the sins of God's people, but because God was so holy and the people were so unclean with sin, there was uncertainty as to whether the High Priest could complete the job and survive being in the presence of such a holy God. This is why God sent

Jesus, who is referred to as the *"better hope"*. He was the better hope because the *"law made nothing perfect"*, and rituals that the High Priests had to perform every year could not suffice; they could not remove the barrier between God and man, allowing us to *"draw near"* to Him (Hebrews 7:19, NIV).

Through Christ's sacrifice by dying on the cross once, He solved the issue of sin once and for all, removed the barrier between us, and reconciled us back to the love and peace of God, our creator. He had in essence paid a ransom for my death with His blood, even though He Himself had done nothing wrong. Romans 6:23 (KJV) clearly states that *"the wages of sin is death"*. However, as the rest of this verse outlines, He had willingly chosen to change the course of my life, by giving me *"the gift of God"*, which is *"eternal life through Jesus Christ our Lord."* Although the gift of an eternal and peaceful life will be redeemed in Heaven, I came to learn that Christ also made this peace available to me, here on Earth (Luke 2:14, NIV).

Oftentimes, we allow our feelings of guilt and shame to create an imaginary barrier between us and God, pulling us further and further away from Him. Once we confess our sins to God, He wants to demonstrate his love and compassion by acting as though the wrong we did never existed in the first place. There is no greater peace than that of starting over with a clean slate and renewed hope in tomorrow. That's what Christ makes accessible for us all today. In starting from the basics, I began to internalise that Christ's love and compassion for me and His demonstration of this on the cross was the ultimate symbol of peace. I am assured that whatever I go through, the sovereign God, who is *"not a man that he should lie"* (Numbers 23:19, KJV) has clearly stated that He *"will never leave you nor forsake you"*, thus I can have peace in the midst of the unknowing (Hebrews 13:5, NKJV). The same is available to you.

Still Running?

The strange thing is that even if we only have a minute awareness of God's offer of love, peace and salvation, a lot of us still choose to run away from Him, instead of experiencing the benefits of drawing closer to Him. It reminds me of our rabbits, called Pumba and Timone; if you have never seen *The Lion King*, it's never too late to get in on the action! When we originally purchased these rabbits after years of begging and bargaining from my husband and the children, the hope was that there would be a sense of closeness between our rabbits and us. After getting over the initial shock of having a pet other than a placid goldfish in our home, we envisioned being able to hold and stroke them, feed them by hand, and keep them safe and warm. Disappointingly, however, we came to find that the opposite was true. Pumba and Timone just don't like to be touched, let alone to be held. When we attempt to be close to them, they run away. They would rather go and hide amongst their urine and faeces than be intimate with us, even though we have the food, shelter and comfort they both require. I often wonder if God feels the same about us. He created us and removed the barrier so we could feel and be close to Him, yet so many of us still run.

In time, I began to understand that when you go to a doctor, you don't go to him 'well' or under the false pretense of having it all together. Moreover, it would certainly be counterproductive to run from a person who could help you. Instead, you go to a doctor because you are sick and you need him to make you better. That's what Jesus Christ did for me; He met and healed me on my road to greatness. I didn't have to be great or 'well' to first come to Him.

As a psychotherapist, pastor and a Christian, I believe that ultimately a dependence on Jesus Christ is the foundation of peace and, without it, these practical or psychotherapeutic tools can only go so far. When this world is going crazy around me, I have often sought something to help me cope that isn't bound by the limits of this realm or the restrictions of my 5 senses. I have always relied on something that will encourage me to look beyond my current vantage point, seeing higher and seeing better despite the odds. My faith in Christ allows me to still believe in the power of a glimmer of light in the midst of the vast mass of darkness being enough to hold me until *"joy comes in the morning"* (Psalm 30:5, NKJV). It is stories like Ronald's that often cause me to reflect deeply on my uphill journey into finding real peace. It ultimately reaffirms that this feeling of being 'held up' during crisis is anchored in nothing else but my spiritual walk and faith in Jesus Christ.

Tips on Starting or Improving Your Own Spiritual Journey

If you are new, alien to Christianity, or just need some fresh ideas and are open to gaining the sense of peace and strength that we have described throughout this book, although none of these are foolproof, here are a few tips on how to start your own spiritual walk with Jesus Christ:

- Pray to God through talking to Him about your innermost thoughts and feelings, asking Him to be with you on this new journey to getting to know Him more.

- Find a good Bible believing and demonstrating church to attend regularly (Check out The Rock Church www.trclondon.org).
- Attend smaller Bible study groups with well-versed yet patient leaders.
- Be mindful of what content you surround yourself with on a daily basis. Consider whether it lifts you up or tears you down.
- Watch or listen to practical yet soul edifying podcasts or sermons online regularly. A few personal recommendations are: Pastor G (from www.trclondon.org), Bishop T. D. Jakes (from www.thepottershouse.org) or Pastor Steven Furtick (www.elevationchurch.org).
- Purchase a good Christian devotional, which normally provides daily examples of faith in action.
- Listen to gospel or worship music online to learn more about the character of Christ and uplift your soul.
- Buy a good and simple study Bible that helps explain otherwise complicated concepts in the Bible, and read this daily.
- Read and re-read this book when peace reminders are needed. Note down or highlight some of the verses listed in your own Bible.
- Surround yourself with Christians who are also on a pursuit of peace and desire to strengthen their spiritual walk with Christ.
- Familiarise yourself with Bible scriptures and, when the opportunity presents itself, put your faith in Christ to the test.
- In the Bible (KJV), there are over 400 references to various forms of peace. Reading them daily, memorising or writing them down provides a much-needed reminder of God's promises, and helps to shift your perspective to peace, despite the uncertain road ahead of you, knowing fully that He is holding you tightly in the palm of His hands. Here are a few Bible scriptures to help get you started:

Peaceful Promises

Psalm 94:19 (GW)

"When I was worried about many things, your assuring words soothed my soul."

Psalm 4:8 (TPT)

"Now, because of you, Lord, I will lie down in peace and sleep comes at once, for no matter what happens, I will live unafraid!"

Psalm 55:18 (TPT)

"Though many wish to fight and the tide of battle turns against me, by your power, I will be safe and secure; peace will be my portion."

In Closing

In closing, the Bible reminds us to *"search for peace, and work to maintain it"* (Psalm 34:14, NLT). This suggests that, as this book has outlined, your pursuit of peace will not be plain sailing and will involve you being a work in progress for some time to come. I trust however that you have been challenged to expand your thinking around your new journey and have been reminded that difficulties along the way do not negate your ability to make it. Whatever changes you do make, make them gradually, leading with intentionality. As you learn and grow, don't forget to share; someone else may need what you are becoming.

Peace is available to us all, but ultimately, I believe that the use of practical and psychotherapeutic techniques alone has their limits. If you include Christ on your journey from pieces to peace, the actualisation of this goal is within your reach. Whilst you undergo your transformation, you can rest assured that like the story of 'the potter and the clay', if the pot appears to be turning out badly, God will simply start over, using the same clay to make another pot, never discarding you or releasing you from the safety of his hands (Jeremiah 18:1-12, MSG).

I will leave you with an invitation: I believe that if you truly find Jesus Christ, in Him, will find lasting peace.

God bless you on your journey from pieces to peace.

References

Antonovsky, A. (1967). Social class, life expectancy and overall mortality. *The Milbank Memorial Fund Quarterly, 45(2),* 31-73.

Baldwin, M. (1987). Interview with Carl Rogers on the use of the self in therapy. In M. Baldwin & V. Satir (Eds.), *The use of the self in therapy* (pp. 45-52). New York: Haworth Press.

Baer, R. A., Smith, G. T., Lykins, E., Button, D., Krietemeyer, J., Sauer, S., ... Williams, J. M. G. (2008). Construct validity of the five facet mindfulness questionnaire in meditating and non-meditating samples. *Assessment, 15*(3), 329-42.

Beck, A. T. (1967). *The diagnosis and management of depression.* Philadelphia, PA: University of Pennsylvania Press.

Beck, A. T. (1976). *Cognitive therapy and the emotional disorders.* New York: Penguin.

Bergin, A. E. (1980). Psychotherapy and religious values. *Journal of Consulting and Clinical Psychology, 48*, 95-105.

Bergin, A. E., & Jensen, J. P. (1990). Religiosity and psychotherapists: A national survey. *Psychotherapy, 27*, 3-7.

Brooks, O. (2009). Tales out of school: Counseling African-Caribbean young people in schools. *Journal of Social Work Practice, 23*(1), 65-67.

Bränström, R., Duncan, L. G., & Moskowitz, J. T. (2011). The association between dispositional mindfulness, psychological well-being and perceived health in a Swedish population-based sample. *British Journal of Health Psychology, 16*(2), 300-316.

Creswell, J. D. (2017). Mindfulness interventions. *Annual Review of Psychology, 68.*

Ellis, A. (1957). Rational psychotherapy and individual psychology. *Journal of Individual Psychology, 13*, 38-44.

Ellis, A. (1962). *Reason and emotion in psychotherapy.* New York: Stuart.

Franklin, A. J. (1999). Invisibility syndrome and racial identity development in psychotherapy and counseling African American men. *The Counseling Psychologist, 27*, 761-793.

Franklin, A. J. (2004). *From brotherhood to manhood: How Black men rescue their relationships and dreams from the invisibility syndrome.* Hoboken, NJ: John Wiley & Sons, Inc.

Franklin, A. J., & Boyd-Franklin, N. (2000). Invisibility syndrome: A clinical model of the effects of racism on African-American males. *American Journal of Orthopsychiatry, 70*, 33-41.

Gray, A. (1994). *An introduction to the therapeutic frame.* London: Routledge.

Gu, J., Strauss, C., Bond, R., & Cavanagh, K. (2015). How do mindfulness-based cognitive therapy and mindfulness-based stress reduction improve mental health and well-being? A systematic review and meta-analysis of mediation studies. *Clinical Psychology Review, 37,* 1-12.

Huckestein, C. R. (2008). For Christian counselors in public schools. *Human Development, 29*(1), 32-34.

Lebow, J. (2006). *Research for the psychotherapist: From science to practice.* London: Routledge.

Lichtenstein, D. (2003). The appearance of the other in the attacks of September 11. In D. Moss (Ed.), *Hating in the first person plural* (pp. 311-323). New York: Other Press.

Mearns, D., & Thorne, B. (2000). *Person-centred therapy today: New frontiers in theory and practice.* London: Sage Publications.

Mindfulness.(n.d.). Retrieved October 12, 2017, from https://en.wikipedia.org/wiki/Mindfulness

Querstret, D., & Cropley, M. (2013). Assessing treatments used to reduce rumination and/or worry: A systematic review. Clinical Psychology Review, 33(8), 996-1009.

Rogers, C. R. (1957). The necessary and sufficient conditions of therapeutic personality change. *Journal of Consulting Psychology, 21*, 95-103.

Williams, M. (2016). *Mindfulness.* Retrieved January 7, 2016, from https://www.nhs.uk/Conditions/stress-anxiety-depression/Pages/mindfulness.aspx

Word, C. O., Zanna, M. P., & Cooper, J. (1974). The nonverbal mediation of self-fulfilling prophecies in interracial interaction. *Journal of Experimental Social Psychology, 10*, 109-120.

About The Author

Selone Ajewole is an experienced psychotherapist with a Certificate in Counselling, a BSc in Psychology and an MSc in Therapeutic Counselling. As a UK counselling professional, she is member of the British Association for Counselling and Psychotherapy (www.bacp.co.uk) and fully adheres to their strict code of ethics. Selone is also a pastor of a spirit-filled yet vibrant and relatable church and charity called The Rock Church in the heart of London's East End. Selone has also co-authored the book *The Colours of Love Relationship Manual*, which sold extremely well on an international scale. Despite all of these achievements, of most importance are the relationships she has cultivated with God, her husband and her precious children. Ultimately, fulfilling her life's purpose as a beacon of hope and light to others is what continues to push her forward, despite the odds.

Notes

FROM PIECES TO PEACE

NOTES

NOTES

NOTES

NOTES

FROM PIECES TO PEACE

NOTES

NOTES